Building Resilience: How Divorce Affects Children's Self-Esteem and Self-Confidence

Copyright Page

TITLE: Building Resilience: How Divorce Affects Children's Self-Esteem and Self-Confidence

1ST Edition

ISBN: 9798223202660

Table of Contents

Building Resilience: How Divorce Affects Children's Self-Esteem and Self-Confidence... 1

Chapter 1: The Effects of A Divorce on The Children 2

Chapter 2: The Psychological Impact of Divorce on Children 10

Chapter 3: The Long-term Effects of Divorce on Children's Relationships 20

Chapter 4: Academic Performance and Divorce: How it Affects Children's Education 30

Chapter 5: Divorce and Its Impact on Children's Emotional Well-being 40

Chapter 6: Divorce and Its Effect on Children's Self-esteem and Self-confidence 48

Chapter 7: Divorce and Its Influence on Children's Social Development 58

Chapter 8: Divorce and Its Impact on Children's Mental Health 66

Chapter 9: Divorce and Its Effect on Children's Attachment Styles ... 75

Chapter 10: Divorce and Its Consequences on Children's Behavior and Discipline 84

Chapter 11: Divorce and Its Influence on Children's Future Romantic Relationships 93

Building Resilience: How Divorce Affects Children's Self-Esteem and Self-Confidence

By Roberto Miguel Rodriguez

Chapter 1: The Effects of A Divorce on The Children

Understanding Divorce and Its Impact on Children

Divorce is a significant life event that can have long-lasting effects on children. As educators, it is crucial to understand the various ways in which divorce can impact children's lives and to support them in navigating these challenges. This subchapter aims to provide insights into the effects of divorce on children's self-esteem, self-confidence, relationships, education, emotional well-being, social development, mental health, attachment styles, behavior, discipline, and future romantic relationships.

When parents divorce, children often experience a range of emotions such as sadness, anger, confusion, and anxiety. These emotions can significantly impact their self-esteem and self-confidence. Educators must be aware of these emotional struggles and create a supportive and understanding environment for children going through divorce.

The psychological impact of divorce on children should not be underestimated. Children may develop depression, anxiety disorders, or exhibit behavioral problems as a result of the divorce. It is important for educators to collaborate with mental health professionals and provide appropriate interventions and support to help children cope with these challenges effectively.

Divorce can also have long-term effects on children's relationships. Research suggests that children of divorced parents may struggle with forming and maintaining healthy relationships later in life. Educators can play a crucial role in providing guidance and teaching essential skills for healthy relationship development.

Moreover, divorce can impact children's academic performance. The stress and emotional turmoil associated with divorce can lead to difficulties in concentrating, lower motivation, and decreased academic achievement. Educators should be mindful of these challenges and provide additional academic support and resources to help children succeed academically.

Furthermore, divorce can have a profound impact on children's emotional well-being. Children may experience feelings of guilt, blame, and even a sense of abandonment. Educators should create a safe space for children to express their emotions and provide opportunities for counseling or therapy if needed.

Divorce can also influence children's social development. They may struggle with making friends, trusting others, or developing healthy social skills. Educators should encourage positive social interactions, foster empathy, and provide opportunities for children to build strong peer relationships.

In conclusion, divorce can have a significant impact on children's lives across various domains. As educators, it is essential to understand these effects and provide appropriate support and resources to help children navigate these challenges successfully. By addressing the effects of divorce on children's self-esteem, relationships, education, emotional well-being, social development, mental health, attachment styles, behavior, discipline, and future romantic relationships, educators can play a vital role in building resilience in children of divorced parents.

Factors Influencing the Effects of Divorce on Children

Divorce is a complex and emotional process that can have a significant impact on children. However, the effects of divorce on children can vary greatly depending on a variety of factors. This subchapter explores the factors that influence how divorce affects children, providing educators with valuable insights to better support their students.

One of the key factors that influence the effects of divorce on children is the age at which the divorce occurs. Younger children may struggle to understand the reasons behind their parents' separation, leading to feelings of confusion and insecurity. They may also experience a disruption in their daily routines and a loss of stability, which can impact their emotional well-being and academic performance. On the other hand, older children may have a better understanding of divorce but may still experience feelings of anger, guilt, and sadness. They may also face additional challenges, such as having to take on more responsibilities or dealing with parental conflict.

The level of parental conflict during and after the divorce is another important factor. High levels of conflict can create a hostile and tense environment for children, leading to increased emotional distress and a negative impact on their self-esteem and self-confidence. Conversely, parents who are able to maintain a cooperative and respectful co-parenting relationship can help mitigate the negative effects of divorce on their children.

The level of support and resources available to children also plays a crucial role. Educators can play a vital role in providing emotional support, creating a safe and nurturing school environment, and connecting children and families with additional resources, such as counseling services or support groups. These resources can help children cope with the challenges of divorce and build resilience.

It is also important to consider the child's own temperament and personality. Some children may be more resilient and adaptable, while others may be more sensitive and vulnerable to the effects of divorce. Understanding and recognizing these individual differences can help educators tailor their support and interventions accordingly.

In conclusion, the effects of divorce on children are influenced by a combination of factors, including the child's age, the level of parental conflict, the available support and resources, and the child's own temperament. By understanding these factors, educators can better support children through the challenges of divorce, promoting their emotional well-being, academic success, and future relationships.

Common Emotional Reactions of Children to Divorce

Divorce is a challenging life event that can have a significant impact on children's emotional well-being and overall development. As educators, it is crucial for us to understand the common emotional reactions that children may have in response to their parents' divorce. By recognizing and addressing these reactions, we can provide the necessary support to help children build resilience and navigate through this difficult time.

One of the most common emotional reactions of children to divorce is sadness and grief. They may experience a profound sense of loss as their family structure changes, and they may mourn the absence of a complete and intact family unit. This sadness can manifest in various ways, such as tearfulness, withdrawal, or a general sense of melancholy.

Children may also feel a sense of guilt and self-blame for their parents' divorce. They may believe that their behavior or actions somehow caused the marital breakdown, leading to feelings of shame and responsibility. Educators can play a vital role in dispelling these misconceptions and reassuring children that divorce is an adult decision that is not their fault.

Anger and frustration are other common emotional reactions that children may exhibit during or after a divorce. They may direct their anger towards their parents, themselves, or even their peers. This anger can stem from feelings of betrayal, abandonment, or a sense of powerlessness. It is important for educators to create a safe and supportive environment where children can express their anger constructively and learn healthy ways to manage their emotions.

Anxiety and fear are also prevalent emotional reactions in children of divorce. They may worry about the uncertainty of their future, changes in their living arrangements, or the impact on their relationships with both parents. Educators can help alleviate these anxieties by providing consistent routines and open communication channels, allowing children to voice their concerns and fears.

Lastly, children may experience a range of conflicting emotions, such as relief and guilt or loyalty and betrayal. They may feel relieved if the divorce has ended a hostile or toxic environment, but at the same time, they may feel guilty for feeling relieved. Additionally, children may struggle with divided loyalties between their parents, leading to feelings of betrayal regardless of the outcome.

Understanding these common emotional reactions can help educators provide a more empathetic and supportive environment for children of divorce. By addressing these emotions, we can help children develop the resilience, self-esteem, and self-confidence needed to navigate through this challenging time and build healthy relationships in the future.

The Role of Parents in Mitigating the Effects of Divorce on Children

Divorce can have a significant impact on children's self-esteem and self-confidence. As educators, it is essential for us to understand the role that parents play in mitigating these effects and supporting children through this challenging time.

First and foremost, parents need to prioritize open communication with their children. This means creating a safe and non-judgmental space where children can express their feelings and concerns.

Encouraging them to talk about their emotions will help them process their experiences and feel validated.

Parents should also strive to maintain a consistent and predictable routine for their children. Divorce can disrupt a child's sense of stability, so it is crucial for parents to establish a structure that provides a sense of security. This includes maintaining regular mealtimes, bedtimes, and extracurricular activities.

Additionally, parents should work together to co-parent effectively. This means putting aside personal differences and focusing on what is best for the children. Consistent rules and boundaries should be established in both households, ensuring that children have a sense of stability and consistency, regardless of which parent they are with.

Parents should also be mindful of the language they use when discussing the divorce. Negative comments or blame-shifting can have a detrimental impact on children's self-esteem. Instead, parents should strive to use positive and constructive language that emphasizes the love and support they have for their children.

Lastly, parents should seek professional help if needed. Divorce can be a challenging and emotional process for both parents and children, and it may be beneficial to involve a therapist or counselor to provide additional support. These professionals can help children navigate their emotions and provide parents with guidance on how to best support their children through this transition.

By understanding the role that parents play in mitigating the effects of divorce on children, educators can better support their students in the classroom. By creating a safe and supportive environment, maintaining consistent routines, encouraging open communication, and seeking professional help when needed, parents can help their children develop resilience and navigate the challenges of divorce.

Seeking Support for Children Coping with Divorce

Divorce can have a profound impact on children, affecting various aspects of their lives, including their self-esteem, self-confidence, relationships, education, emotional well-being, social development, mental health, attachment styles, behavior, discipline, and even their future romantic relationships. As educators, it is crucial for us to understand these effects and provide the necessary support to help children cope with the challenges they may face during this difficult time.

One of the primary ways we can support children coping with divorce is by creating a safe and nurturing environment within the school setting. This includes fostering open communication and providing a supportive network of teachers, counselors, and other staff members who can listen and offer guidance. By offering a non-judgmental space for children to express their emotions and concerns, we can help them feel validated and understood.

It is also essential to educate ourselves about the psychological impact of divorce on children. By familiarizing ourselves with the common reactions and behaviors exhibited by children going through a divorce, we can better identify and address their needs. This knowledge will enable us to provide targeted interventions and resources to support their emotional well-being.

Academic performance can often be negatively affected by divorce. As educators, we can work closely with parents and guardians to create a supportive educational plan for the child. This may involve setting realistic academic goals, providing additional academic assistance, or even implementing a flexible schedule to accommodate the child's emotional needs.

Furthermore, promoting positive social interactions and helping children develop healthy coping mechanisms can have a significant impact on their social development. By teaching them effective communication skills, conflict resolution strategies, and empathy, we can empower children to build and maintain healthy relationships with their peers.

Finally, it is crucial to recognize that the effects of divorce can be long-lasting and may impact children's future romantic relationships. By providing them with appropriate guidance and support, we can help them develop a secure attachment style and foster healthy relationships in the future.

In conclusion, as educators, we have a vital role to play in supporting children coping with divorce. By creating a safe and nurturing environment, educating ourselves about the effects of divorce, addressing academic challenges, promoting healthy social development, and preparing children for their future relationships, we can help build resilience in children and empower them to navigate the challenges they may face.

Chapter 2: The Psychological Impact of Divorce on Children

Understanding the Psychological Effects of Divorce on Children

Divorce is a challenging experience for everyone involved, but it can have particularly profound psychological effects on children. As educators, it is crucial for us to understand these effects and provide the necessary support to help children navigate through this difficult time.

One of the most immediate and noticeable effects of divorce on children is the emotional impact. Children may experience a wide range of emotions such as sadness, anger, confusion, and anxiety. These emotions can affect their overall well-being and their ability to concentrate and engage in their academic work. It is important to create a safe and supportive environment in the classroom where children feel comfortable expressing their emotions and seeking help when needed.

Divorce can also have long-term effects on children's relationships. Children from divorced families may struggle with forming and maintaining healthy relationships in the future. They may have trust issues, fear of commitment, or difficulty in expressing their emotions. As educators, we can help children develop healthy relationship skills by teaching empathy, effective communication, and conflict resolution strategies.

Academic performance can also be significantly impacted by divorce. Children may experience a decline in their academic performance due to the emotional distress they are going through. They may have difficulty concentrating, completing assignments, and participating in class. It is essential to provide additional academic support and understanding during this time, allowing children to catch up and regain their focus.

Divorce can have a profound impact on a child's self-esteem and self-confidence. Children may blame themselves for their parents' separation, leading to feelings of guilt and shame. As educators, it is vital to foster a positive and supportive environment that encourages children to develop a healthy sense of self-worth and resilience.

Furthermore, divorce can influence a child's social development. They may struggle with making friends, feel isolated or rejected, or exhibit aggressive or withdrawn behaviors. As educators, we can promote a sense of belonging and inclusion in the classroom, encouraging positive social interactions and providing opportunities for children to engage in collaborative activities.

Divorce can also impact a child's mental health. They may experience depression, anxiety, or even develop more severe mental health disorders. It is essential to be aware of these signs and symptoms and provide appropriate resources and referrals to mental health professionals when necessary.

Additionally, divorce can affect a child's attachment style. They may struggle with forming secure attachments and trusting others. As educators, we can provide a sense of stability and consistency in the classroom, promoting healthy attachments and building trust with our students.

Finally, divorce can have long-term consequences on a child's behavior and discipline. They may act out, exhibit aggression, or engage in risky behaviors. It is crucial to set clear expectations and boundaries while also providing support and understanding to help children navigate through their emotions and behaviors.

Ultimately, as educators, we play a critical role in supporting children from divorced families. By understanding the psychological effects of divorce on children, we can create a nurturing and empathetic environment that fosters resilience, self-esteem, and healthy relationships.

Emotional and Behavioral Changes in Children after Divorce

Divorce can have a profound impact on children's emotional and behavioral well-being. Understanding these changes is crucial for educators who play a vital role in supporting children affected by divorce. This subchapter explores the emotional and behavioral changes that children may experience after their parents' divorce.

One of the most common emotional changes observed in children after divorce is a sense of loss and sadness. They may feel a deep sense of grief for the loss of their intact family and struggle to adjust to the new reality. These feelings can manifest in various ways, such as increased tearfulness, withdrawal, or expressions of anger. Educators need to create a safe and supportive environment where children can express and process their emotions.

Behavioral changes are also common in children after divorce. Some children may exhibit regressive behaviors, such as bedwetting or thumb-sucking, as a way to cope with the stress and uncertainty. Others may become more defiant or exhibit attention-seeking behaviors. These changes in behavior can impact their academic performance and social interactions.

Moreover, divorce can significantly affect children's self-esteem and self-confidence. The disruption of their family structure may lead to feelings of insecurity and a diminished sense of self-worth. Educators can help by providing opportunities for children to build their self-esteem through praise, encouragement, and recognizing their strengths and achievements.

Children of divorce may also experience difficulties in developing healthy relationships, both in the present and in the future. They may struggle with trust and intimacy, fearing that relationships will end in separation. Educators can support children by promoting healthy relationship skills, such as effective communication, empathy, and conflict resolution.

Additionally, divorce can impact children's academic performance. The stress and emotional upheaval may lead to a decline in their concentration and motivation. Educators should be aware of these potential challenges and provide additional support, such as counseling or academic accommodations, to help mitigate the negative impact on their education.

In conclusion, divorce can trigger a range of emotional and behavioral changes in children. Educators must be sensitive to these changes and provide the necessary support to help children navigate through this challenging time. By understanding the effects of divorce on children's emotional well-being, educators can play a crucial role in building their resilience and promoting their overall development.

Coping Mechanisms and Resilience in Children of Divorce

Introduction:

Divorce is a challenging experience for children, impacting various aspects of their lives. In this subchapter, we will explore coping mechanisms and resilience in children of divorce. Understanding these concepts is crucial for educators working with children affected by divorce, as it can help support their emotional well-being, academic performance, and future relationships.

1. The Effects of Divorce on Children's Coping Mechanisms:

Divorce often introduces uncertainty, stress, and emotional turmoil into children's lives. As educators, it is essential to recognize the various coping mechanisms children may adopt to navigate these challenges. Some children may seek support from friends, while others may withdraw or express their emotions through art or writing. By identifying these coping strategies, educators can provide appropriate support and encourage healthy ways of expression.

2. Building Resilience in Children of Divorce:

Resilience is the ability to bounce back from adversity and develop a positive outlook despite difficult circumstances. Educators play a vital role in fostering resilience in children of divorce. By creating a safe and supportive environment, educators can empower children to develop coping skills, build self-esteem, and cultivate a sense of control over their lives. Encouraging open communication, providing opportunities for expression, and promoting a growth mindset are essential strategies to enhance resilience.

3. Supporting Academic Performance:

Divorce can significantly impact children's education. Educators can help mitigate the negative effects by providing a supportive and understanding classroom environment. By fostering a sense of belonging and tailoring teaching methods to individual needs, educators can help children regain focus and motivation. Collaborating with parents and offering additional resources, such as counseling or tutoring, can further support children's academic success.

4. Nurturing Emotional Well-being:

Divorce can lead to emotional challenges, including sadness, anger, and anxiety. Educators can create a nurturing space where children feel comfortable expressing their emotions. Implementing social-emotional learning programs and teaching coping strategies can help children regulate their emotions and develop resilience. Encouraging healthy relationships among peers and providing opportunities for self-reflection can also contribute to emotional well-being.

5. Promoting Positive Relationships:

Divorce can influence children's future relationships. Educators can help children develop healthy relationship skills by modeling positive interactions, promoting empathy, and teaching conflict resolution strategies. Building a sense of community within the classroom can also provide children with a supportive network that fosters positive social development.

Conclusion:

Coping mechanisms and resilience are vital aspects of supporting children of divorce. As educators, understanding the effects of divorce on children's self-esteem, self-confidence, academic performance, and relationships is crucial. By cultivating resilience, providing a supportive environment, and teaching coping strategies, educators can help children navigate the challenges of divorce and build a strong foundation for their future well-being.

Psychological Interventions to Support Children through Divorce

Divorce is a significant life event that can have a profound impact on children's well-being and overall development. As educators, it is crucial to understand the psychological interventions that can support children through this challenging period in their lives. By implementing these strategies, we can help promote resilience and mitigate the negative effects of divorce on children.

One effective intervention is providing a safe and supportive environment within the school setting. Children going through divorce may feel overwhelmed, confused, and emotionally fragile. Creating a nurturing atmosphere where they feel understood, validated, and cared for can greatly contribute to their emotional well-being.

Another crucial intervention is fostering open communication. Encouraging children to express their thoughts and feelings about the divorce can help them process their emotions and gain a sense of control over their situation. Teachers can provide age-appropriate opportunities for children to share their experiences, such as journaling, group discussions, or one-on-one conversations.

Furthermore, teaching coping skills and emotional regulation techniques is essential for children navigating divorce. Helping children develop effective strategies to manage stress, anxiety, and other negative emotions can empower them to cope with the challenges they may encounter. This can include teaching deep breathing exercises, mindfulness techniques, or engaging in creative activities that promote self-expression.

Collaboration with parents and other professionals involved in the child's life is also crucial. By working together, educators can gain a comprehensive understanding of the child's needs and tailor interventions accordingly. This collaboration can involve regular communication, sharing resources, and coordinating efforts to create consistency and support across different settings.

Lastly, it is essential to provide ongoing support and monitor children's progress over time. Regular check-ins, individualized attention, and referrals to mental health professionals when needed can ensure that children receive the necessary support and intervention throughout their journey.

By implementing these psychological interventions, educators can play a vital role in supporting children through divorce. By fostering resilience, promoting emotional well-being, and providing a safe and supportive environment, we can help children navigate this challenging period and minimize the long-term impact of divorce on their lives. Together, we can empower children to develop healthy coping mechanisms, build positive relationships, and thrive despite the challenges they may face.

Promoting Positive Mental Health in Children of Divorce

Introduction:

Divorce can have a significant impact on children's mental health, leading to various emotional challenges and affecting their overall well-being. As educators, it is crucial for us to understand these effects and work towards promoting positive mental health in children of divorce. This subchapter aims to provide insights and strategies to support children through this difficult time and help them build resilience.

Understanding the Psychological Impact:

Children of divorce often experience feelings of sadness, anger, confusion, and abandonment. These emotions can have long-term consequences on their psychological well-being, including increased anxiety, depression, and lowered self-esteem. Educators must recognize these signs and respond empathetically to create a supportive environment.

Creating a Supportive Classroom Environment:

1. Open Communication: Encourage open dialogue about divorce, allowing children to express their feelings and concerns without

judgment. Provide opportunities for them to share their experiences through journaling or group discussions.

2. Empathy and Validation: Show understanding and empathy towards children's emotions. Validate their experiences and reassure them that their feelings are valid and normal.

3. Building Resilience: Teach children coping mechanisms to deal with stress and adversity. Promote problem-solving skills, positive self-talk, and mindfulness techniques to enhance their resilience.

Collaborating with Parents:

1. Parental Involvement: Communicate with parents regularly to understand the child's home environment and any ongoing challenges. Collaborate on strategies to support the child's emotional well-being.

2. Referral to Counseling Services: Identify children who may require professional support and refer them to school counselors or external mental health services. Ensure all children have access to the necessary resources.

Incorporating Social and Emotional Learning (SEL):

1. SEL Curriculum: Implement a comprehensive SEL program that addresses emotional regulation, empathy, and relationship-building skills. This will provide children with tools to manage their emotions and develop positive relationships.

2. Peer Support Groups: Organize support groups where children can connect with peers experiencing similar challenges. These groups provide a safe space for sharing experiences and building resilience together.

Conclusion:

Promoting positive mental health in children of divorce requires a collaborative effort from educators, parents, and the wider community. By understanding the psychological impact, creating a supportive environment, collaborating with parents, and incorporating SEL strategies, we can help children navigate the challenges of divorce, build resilience, and thrive academically and socially. Together, we can make a difference in their lives, enabling them to develop healthy relationships and a positive outlook on their future romantic relationships.

Chapter 3: The Long-term Effects of Divorce on Children's Relationships

Impact of Divorce on Parent-Child Relationships

Divorce is a complex and multifaceted experience that affects not only the couple involved but also their children. One of the most significant areas impacted by divorce is the parent-child relationship. Educators play a crucial role in understanding and supporting children who have experienced divorce, as they can provide valuable insights and guidance to help navigate the challenges that arise.

The Effects of A Divorce on The Children

Divorce can have a profound impact on children's emotional well-being, self-esteem, and self-confidence. It disrupts their sense of stability and security, causing feelings of sadness, anger, and confusion. Children may also experience a sense of guilt or blame themselves for their parents' separation. Educators need to be aware of these effects and provide a supportive environment where children can express their feelings and concerns.

The Psychological Impact of Divorce on Children

Divorce can lead to a range of psychological issues in children, including anxiety, depression, and low self-esteem. These challenges can hinder their academic performance and social development. Educators should be mindful of these potential psychological consequences and work closely with parents and other professionals to provide appropriate support and resources.

The Long-Term Effects of Divorce on Children's Relationships

Divorce can have long-lasting effects on children's relationships, both romantic and non-romantic. They may struggle with trust issues, fear of abandonment, or difficulties in forming secure attachments. Educators can help by fostering healthy relationships and providing guidance on conflict resolution and effective communication skills.

Academic Performance and Divorce: How it Affects Children's Education

Divorce can disrupt children's academic performance due to the emotional turmoil and instability it brings. They may have difficulty concentrating, completing assignments, or participating in class. Educators can offer additional support, such as individualized attention or counseling, to help children cope with these challenges and maintain their academic progress.

Divorce and its Impact on Children's Emotional Well-being

Divorce can significantly impact children's emotional well-being, leading to increased stress, anxiety, and a range of emotional difficulties. Educators should be vigilant in identifying signs of emotional distress and provide a safe and supportive environment where children can express their emotions and seek help if needed.

Divorce and its Effect on Children's Self-esteem and Self-confidence

Divorce can have a detrimental effect on children's self-esteem and self-confidence. They may internalize feelings of rejection and inadequacy, leading to a negative self-image. Educators can counteract these effects by promoting a positive and inclusive classroom environment that fosters self-esteem and self-confidence.

Divorce and its Influence on Children's Social Development

Divorce can disrupt children's social development, as they may struggle with forming and maintaining friendships. They may experience feelings of isolation or difficulty trusting others. Educators can facilitate social interactions, encourage peer support, and provide opportunities for children to develop social skills and build positive relationships.

Divorce and its Impact on Children's Mental Health

Divorce can significantly impact children's mental health, leading to an increased risk of developing mental health disorders such as depression and anxiety. Educators should be trained to recognize signs of mental distress and collaborate with parents and mental health professionals to provide appropriate support and interventions.

Divorce and its Effect on Children's Attachment Styles

Divorce can influence children's attachment styles, affecting their ability to form secure and healthy attachments with others. Educators can promote secure attachments by providing consistency, stability, and nurturing relationships within the school environment.

Divorce and its Consequences on Children's Behavior and Discipline

Divorce can lead to changes in children's behavior and discipline, as they may act out or exhibit challenging behaviors as a result of the emotional upheaval. Educators should employ positive discipline strategies, offer clear boundaries, and provide emotional support to help children navigate these changes.

Divorce and its Influence on Children's Future Romantic Relationships

Divorce can shape children's perspectives and expectations of romantic relationships. They may struggle with trust, commitment, or have difficulty maintaining healthy relationships. Educators can help by fostering open discussions about relationships, modeling healthy behaviors, and providing guidance on building and maintaining positive relationships.

In conclusion, divorce has a profound impact on parent-child relationships, affecting various aspects of children's lives. Educators play a vital role in understanding and supporting children who have experienced divorce, as they can provide valuable guidance and resources to help children navigate the challenges they face. By addressing the impact of divorce on parent-child relationships, educators can help promote resilience and positive outcomes for children.

Effects of Divorce on Sibling Relationships

Divorce is a significant life event that can have far-reaching effects on children's lives, including their relationships with their siblings. Sibling relationships are often the longest-lasting relationships children have, and they play a crucial role in their social and emotional development. Understanding the effects of divorce on sibling relationships is essential for educators to support children as they navigate through this challenging experience.

One of the primary effects of divorce on sibling relationships is a shift in dynamics. Divorce often leads to changes in living arrangements, which can result in siblings living apart or spending less time together. This physical separation can strain the bond between siblings, as they may no longer have the same opportunities for shared experiences and interactions. It can also lead to feelings of loneliness and isolation, as siblings may no longer have each other for emotional support during this tumultuous time.

Furthermore, the emotional impact of divorce on children can also affect their relationships with their siblings. Children may experience feelings of anger, sadness, or confusion about the divorce, which can manifest in their interactions with their siblings. Sibling rivalry and conflict may increase as children try to process their own emotions and cope with the changes in their family dynamics.

It is important for educators to create a supportive environment where children can express their feelings about the divorce and their relationships with their siblings. Providing opportunities for open communication and emotional expression can help children navigate the challenges they may face in their sibling relationships. Educators can also facilitate sibling bonding activities and encourage cooperation and empathy between siblings to strengthen their relationship.

Additionally, educators can play a vital role in promoting resilience in children experiencing the effects of divorce on their sibling relationships. By providing resources and guidance on coping strategies, educators can help children develop the necessary skills to navigate through this difficult time. They can also collaborate with parents and other professionals to ensure a holistic approach to supporting children's well-being.

In conclusion, divorce can have a significant impact on sibling relationships. The physical separation and emotional turmoil that often accompany divorce can strain the bond between siblings and lead to increased conflict. Educators can support children by creating a supportive environment, facilitating open communication, and promoting resilience. By understanding the effects of divorce on sibling relationships, educators can play a crucial role in helping children navigate through this challenging life transition and maintain healthy sibling connections.

Building Healthy Relationships with Extended Family after Divorce

Divorce can have a significant impact on children's relationships, including their relationships with extended family members. As educators, it is important to understand the challenges that children face in maintaining these relationships and to provide support and guidance to help them build healthy connections with their extended family after a divorce.

Extended family members, such as grandparents, aunts, uncles, and cousins, play a crucial role in a child's life. They provide additional sources of love, support, and stability, which can be especially important during and after a divorce. However, divorce can often strain these relationships, as family dynamics change and tensions arise.

One way educators can help children build healthy relationships with their extended family is by encouraging open and honest communication. It is important for children to feel comfortable expressing their emotions and needs to their extended family members. Educators can provide guidance on effective communication strategies and help children find the words to express their feelings.

Another important aspect of building healthy relationships with extended family after divorce is setting boundaries. Divorce can create complex family dynamics, and it is important for children to have a sense of stability and security. Educators can help children establish boundaries with their extended family members, ensuring that their needs and well-being are prioritized.

Furthermore, educators can support children in maintaining a sense of continuity and connection with their extended family. This can be done through activities that involve extended family members, such as family gatherings, holiday celebrations, or even virtual meetings. By promoting these interactions, educators can help children maintain and strengthen their relationships with their extended family.

Additionally, educators can provide resources and support to extended family members themselves. Divorce can be a challenging time for everyone involved, and by offering guidance and resources, educators can help extended family members navigate their own emotions and provide the support that children need.

Building healthy relationships with extended family after divorce is crucial for children's overall well-being and development. By understanding the challenges that children face in maintaining these relationships and providing support and guidance, educators can play a vital role in helping children build resilience and foster positive connections with their extended family members.

Overall, educators have the opportunity to make a significant impact on the lives of children of divorce by promoting healthy relationships with their extended family. By fostering communication, setting boundaries, supporting continuity, and providing resources, educators can help children navigate the complexities of divorce and build strong, lasting connections with their extended family members.

Navigating Co-parenting and Its Influence on Children's Relationships

Co-parenting is a critical aspect of a child's life when their parents go through a divorce. It refers to the joint effort of both parents to raise their children together, even though they are no longer in a romantic relationship. This subchapter will explore the impact of co-parenting on children's relationships and provide guidance for educators on how to support children in navigating these dynamics.

Co-parenting plays a crucial role in shaping the relationships children form with others. When parents can effectively co-parent, children experience stability, consistency, and a sense of security. This, in turn, positively influences their relationships with peers, teachers, and mentors. However, when co-parenting is fraught with conflict, inconsistency, or lack of communication, children may struggle to form healthy relationships with others.

Educators have a unique opportunity to support children in navigating the challenges of co-parenting. By fostering open communication with parents and being aware of the family dynamics, educators can create a safe and supportive environment for children affected by divorce. They can also provide resources, such as counseling services or referrals to external support systems, to help children cope with any emotional or psychological difficulties they may face.

It is important for educators to understand the long-term effects of divorce on children's relationships. Research shows that children from divorced families may have more difficulty forming and maintaining romantic relationships in adulthood. By acknowledging this, educators can implement strategies that promote healthy relationship skills and teach children how to navigate conflict and communicate effectively.

Additionally, educators should be aware of the potential academic impacts of divorce on children's education. Divorce can disrupt a child's routine and lead to emotional distress, which may manifest in decreased academic performance. By providing a supportive and understanding learning environment, educators can help children overcome these challenges and excel academically.

Ultimately, co-parenting significantly influences children's relationships with others, including their social development, emotional well-being, and future romantic relationships. Educators have a critical role in supporting children through these challenges and can make a lasting impact on their overall resilience and well-being. By understanding the effects of divorce on children and their relationships, educators can provide the necessary guidance and support to help children thrive despite the challenges they may face.

Helping Children Form Healthy Relationships in Adulthood after Divorce

Divorce can have a significant impact on children's ability to form healthy relationships in adulthood. As educators, it is crucial for us to understand the long-term effects of divorce on children's relationships and provide them with the necessary support to build resilience and navigate their future romantic relationships successfully.

The effects of a divorce on children can be profound, with many experiencing feelings of sadness, anger, and confusion. These emotions can have a lasting impact on their psychological well-being and influence their ability to trust and form healthy attachments with others. It is essential to create a safe and supportive environment in schools where children can express their emotions and receive guidance from trusted adults.

Divorce can also affect children's academic performance, as they may struggle to concentrate or feel overwhelmed by the changes in their family dynamics. Educators can play a vital role in identifying any academic difficulties and providing appropriate interventions to support these children academically. By offering additional academic resources, counseling services, or creating a flexible learning environment, educators can help children overcome these challenges and thrive academically.

Furthermore, divorce can have a significant impact on children's emotional well-being, self-esteem, and self-confidence. Educators should focus on promoting a positive self-image and fostering a sense of belonging among these children. By providing them with opportunities to succeed, recognizing their strengths, and encouraging them to engage in extracurricular activities, educators can help boost their self-esteem and confidence.

Divorce can also influence children's social development and their ability to form healthy relationships with peers. Educators can facilitate social skills development by promoting teamwork, cooperation, and empathy in the classroom. Encouraging open communication, conflict resolution, and teaching emotional intelligence can also help children develop the necessary skills to establish and maintain healthy relationships in adulthood.

It is crucial to recognize that divorce can impact children's mental health and attachment styles. Educators should collaborate with mental health professionals to identify any signs of emotional distress or attachment difficulties and provide appropriate support or referrals. By creating a nurturing and inclusive environment, educators can help children develop secure attachment styles and promote their mental well-being.

In conclusion, divorce can have a profound impact on children's ability to form healthy relationships in adulthood. As educators, we have a responsibility to understand these long-term effects and provide the necessary support to help children build resilience and develop the skills needed for successful future relationships. By creating a safe and supportive environment, promoting positive self-esteem and social development, and collaborating with mental health professionals, we can assist children in navigating the challenges of divorce and fostering healthy relationships in their adult lives.

Chapter 4: Academic Performance and Divorce: How it Affects Children's Education

Academic Challenges Faced by Children of Divorce

Introduction:

Divorce can have a profound impact on children's lives, including their academic performance. As educators, it is crucial to understand and address the academic challenges faced by children of divorce. This subchapter will explore the various ways in which divorce can affect children's education and provide strategies to support their academic resilience.

1. Disrupted Routine and Stability:

One significant challenge for children of divorce is the disruption of their daily routine and stability. The transition from one household to another can lead to inconsistent schedules, changing schools, and unfamiliar environments. These disruptions can create a sense of instability that affects children's ability to concentrate and engage in their academic tasks.

2. Emotional Distress and Mental Health:

Divorce often brings emotional distress for children, including feelings of sadness, anger, and anxiety. These emotional challenges can have a direct impact on their ability to focus on their studies, leading to decreased academic performance. Educators must be aware of the signs of emotional distress and provide appropriate support, such as counseling or referral to mental health professionals.

3. Lack of Parental Involvement:

Divorce can sometimes result in decreased parental involvement in a child's education. With parents living separately, communication and collaboration between them and the school may become challenging. This lack of parental involvement can hinder a child's academic progress. Educators can mitigate this challenge by actively engaging both parents in the child's education, through regular communication, parent-teacher meetings, and involving them in decision-making processes.

4. Financial Instability:

Divorce often brings financial challenges, which can affect a child's access to educational resources and opportunities. Limited financial resources may result in fewer extracurricular activities, tutoring, or educational materials. Educators can bridge this gap by providing additional resources or connecting families to community support services.

5. Social and Peer Relationships:

Divorce can impact children's social development and peer relationships. They may experience difficulties in building and maintaining friendships, leading to feelings of isolation and low self-esteem. Educators should create a supportive and inclusive classroom environment that fosters positive social interactions and encourages empathy and understanding among students.

Conclusion:

Children of divorce face unique academic challenges that require the support and understanding of educators. By being aware of these challenges, educators can provide targeted support, create a nurturing environment, and work collaboratively with parents to ensure the academic resilience of children of divorce. By addressing these challenges effectively, educators can make a positive impact on the long-term academic success and well-being of these children, helping them build resilience and thrive in their educational journeys.

Factors Affecting Educational Attainment after Divorce

Divorce is a significant life event that can have far-reaching consequences for children, including their educational attainment. As educators, it is crucial to understand the various factors that can affect a child's educational journey after their parents' divorce. By recognizing these factors, we can better support and guide children through this challenging period. This subchapter aims to explore the key elements influencing educational attainment after divorce and provide strategies for educators to promote resilience and academic success.

One of the primary factors affecting educational attainment after divorce is the level of parental involvement in a child's education. Research consistently shows that children with involved parents are more likely to succeed academically. However, divorce often disrupts the traditional family structure, and parents may struggle to maintain the same level of involvement. Educators can play a vital role by fostering open communication with both parents, encouraging their active participation in school activities, and providing resources for co-parenting strategies.

Another critical factor is the emotional well-being of the child. Divorce can lead to increased stress, anxiety, and depression in children, which can negatively impact their academic performance. It is crucial for educators to be aware of these emotional challenges and provide a supportive and empathetic environment. Implementing social-emotional learning programs, offering counseling services, and promoting a positive classroom atmosphere can contribute to children's emotional well-being and, consequently, their educational success.

Additionally, the economic impact of divorce can significantly affect a child's educational opportunities. Financial instability resulting from divorce may limit access to quality education, extracurricular activities, and educational resources. Educators can assist by identifying and connecting families with available financial assistance programs, scholarships, or community resources. Creating an inclusive and equitable learning environment can also help mitigate the impact of economic disparities on educational attainment.

Lastly, the level of conflict between parents during and after divorce can have detrimental effects on a child's academic progress. High levels of conflict can create a hostile and unstable home environment, leading to increased distractions and disruptions in a child's education. Educators can collaborate with parents to promote effective communication, conflict resolution skills, and co-parenting strategies. Encouraging parents to prioritize the child's well-being and providing resources for professional support can contribute to a more stable and conducive learning environment.

In conclusion, several factors can influence a child's educational attainment after their parents' divorce. By understanding these factors and implementing appropriate strategies, educators can support children in overcoming the challenges associated with divorce and promote their resilience and academic success. Ultimately, the goal is to empower children to thrive academically, despite the difficulties they may face due to their parents' divorce.

Strategies for Supporting Children's Education during Divorce

Introduction:

Divorce can have a significant impact on children's education, affecting their academic performance, emotional well-being, self-esteem, and social development. As educators, it is crucial to understand the challenges these children face and implement strategies to support their educational journey during this difficult time. This subchapter explores various strategies that educators can employ to help children navigate their education during and after a divorce.

1. Open Communication and Active Listening:

Establishing open lines of communication with children and their parents is essential. Encourage parents to share information about the divorce's impact on their child's education, any changes in living arrangements, and other relevant details. Actively listen to children's concerns and validate their feelings, providing a safe space for them to express their emotions.

2. Collaborate with Parents and Guardians:

Maintain regular communication with parents or guardians to stay informed about the child's progress, emotional well-being, and any changes in their behavior or academic performance. Collaborate with parents to develop an individualized plan to address the child's unique needs, considering any challenges they might be facing due to the divorce.

3. Provide Academic Support:

Offer additional academic support, such as tutoring or counseling services, to help children cope with any difficulties they may encounter during the divorce. Keep an eye out for signs of declining academic performance and intervene early to prevent further setbacks.

4. Foster a Supportive Classroom Environment:

Create a supportive and inclusive classroom environment that promotes empathy, understanding, and respect. Encourage classmates to be supportive and understanding towards their peers who may be experiencing the effects of divorce. Promote teamwork and collaboration to help children form positive relationships and enhance their social development.

5. Monitor and Address Emotional Well-being:

Pay attention to signs of emotional distress or changes in behavior that may arise from the divorce. Be aware of potential symptoms of anxiety, depression, or withdrawal and provide appropriate support and resources. Collaborate with school counselors, psychologists, or other professionals to address any mental health concerns.

6. Maintain Consistency and Routine:

Children often thrive in structured environments. During and after a divorce, providing a consistent and predictable routine can help children feel more secure and focused on their education. Communicate with parents to maintain consistency in expectations, homework, and classroom activities, even amidst changing family dynamics.

Conclusion:

By implementing these strategies, educators can help mitigate the negative impact of divorce on children's education. By providing support, fostering a positive and inclusive environment, and maintaining open lines of communication, educators can play a vital role in building resilience and promoting the academic success and well-being of children affected by divorce.

Collaborating with Educators to Enhance Academic Resilience

As educators, you play a vital role in supporting children who have experienced divorce and its subsequent impact on their academic resilience. By understanding the effects of divorce on children's self-esteem, self-confidence, and overall well-being, you can help create a safe and nurturing environment that promotes their academic success.

The psychological impact of divorce on children can be significant and long-lasting. Children may experience feelings of sadness, anger, and confusion, which can affect their ability to concentrate and engage in learning. By recognizing these emotions and providing a supportive and empathetic space, educators can help children process their emotions and create a sense of stability in the classroom.

Academic performance can also be affected by divorce. Children may struggle with maintaining focus, completing assignments, or participating in class discussions. By collaborating with parents and guardians, educators can gain valuable insights into the child's home situation and work together to provide necessary support. This can include creating a consistent routine, offering additional academic resources, or providing extra guidance and encouragement.

Divorce can have a profound impact on children's emotional well-being, self-esteem, and self-confidence. Educators can contribute to building resilience by fostering a positive and inclusive classroom environment. This can be achieved through promoting open communication, encouraging peer support, and recognizing and celebrating each child's unique strengths and abilities.

Children's social development may also be influenced by divorce. Educators can help by facilitating opportunities for social interaction, promoting teamwork, and encouraging healthy relationships among peers. By creating a sense of belonging and community within the classroom, educators can support children in developing strong social skills and positive relationships with their peers.

Furthermore, divorce can affect children's mental health and attachment styles. Educators can collaborate with mental health professionals to identify and address any mental health concerns that may arise. By providing access to appropriate resources and interventions, educators can help children develop healthy coping strategies and build resilience.

Lastly, divorce can impact children's behavior and discipline. By implementing consistent and fair disciplinary practices, educators can help children understand boundaries and expectations. By addressing any behavioral challenges promptly and providing appropriate support, educators can foster positive behavior and create a conducive learning environment.

In conclusion, collaborating with educators is crucial in enhancing the academic resilience of children affected by divorce. By understanding the various effects of divorce on children, educators can create a supportive and nurturing environment that promotes their academic success and overall well-being. Through open communication, collaboration with parents, and access to necessary resources, educators can play a vital role in helping children navigate the challenges of divorce and thrive academically and emotionally. By working together, we can empower children to overcome adversity and build a brighter future for themselves.

Promoting Educational Success and Future Opportunities for Children of Divorce

Divorce is a challenging experience for children, and it can have long-lasting effects on their overall well-being, including their educational success and future opportunities. As educators, it is crucial to understand the specific needs of children of divorce and provide them with the necessary support to thrive academically and socially. By recognizing and addressing the unique challenges they face, we can help these children build resilience and ensure a brighter future for them.

One of the most significant effects of divorce on children is the impact it has on their emotional well-being. Many children of divorce may experience feelings of sadness, anxiety, and confusion, which can hinder their ability to concentrate and learn. It is important for educators to create a safe and supportive environment where these children feel comfortable expressing their emotions and seeking help when needed. By offering counseling services or partnering with mental health professionals, schools can provide the necessary resources to address the psychological impact of divorce on children.

Academic performance is another area that can be affected by divorce. Children of divorce may face additional stressors and disruptions in their daily lives, which can lead to a decline in their academic performance. As educators, we can play a crucial role in supporting these children by providing additional academic assistance, such as tutoring or extra resources, to help them stay on track. Additionally, open communication between teachers, parents, and students can ensure that any challenges are addressed promptly, allowing children to receive the necessary support.

Divorce can also influence children's social development and future relationships. Some children may struggle with forming healthy attachments or have difficulties trusting others due to the breakdown of their parents' relationship. Educators can help children develop healthy social skills by promoting inclusive and supportive classroom environments. Encouraging collaboration, empathy, and communication among students can help children of divorce build positive relationships and develop the necessary skills for future romantic relationships.

Ultimately, promoting educational success and future opportunities for children of divorce requires a holistic approach. By providing emotional support, academic assistance, and fostering healthy social development, educators can empower these children to overcome the challenges they face and achieve their full potential. Together, we can build resilience in children of divorce and ensure they have the tools they need to succeed academically and in their future endeavors.

Chapter 5: Divorce and Its Impact on Children's Emotional Well-being

Emotional Challenges Experienced by Children of Divorce

Divorce is a life-altering event that can have a profound impact on children's emotional well-being. As educators, it is crucial for us to understand and address the emotional challenges these children face in order to support their resilience and overall development.

One of the primary emotional challenges experienced by children of divorce is a sense of loss and grief. The dissolution of their parents' marriage can be extremely distressing, and children may mourn the loss of their intact family. They may experience feelings of sadness, anger, and confusion, and struggle to come to terms with the new family dynamic.

Another emotional challenge is anxiety and fear. Children of divorce often worry about the future and the stability of their relationships with both parents. They may feel uncertain about their own place in the family and fear abandonment. These anxieties can impact their ability to concentrate and engage in school, leading to academic difficulties.

Divorce can also affect children's self-esteem and self-confidence. They may blame themselves for the breakup, believing that their actions or behavior caused the separation. This can result in feelings of guilt, shame, and a diminished sense of self-worth. As educators, it is essential to provide a supportive and nurturing environment that helps rebuild their self-esteem and instills a positive self-image.

Furthermore, children of divorce may struggle with their social development. They may find it challenging to form and maintain friendships, as they may fear rejection or experience difficulties in trusting others. It is important for educators to create a safe and inclusive classroom environment that fosters healthy relationships and encourages empathy and understanding among peers.

Additionally, the emotional challenges experienced by children of divorce can have long-term effects on their future romantic relationships. Research suggests that they may have a higher likelihood of experiencing relationship difficulties and divorce themselves. By providing education and support around healthy relationship skills, educators can help mitigate these long-term effects and promote healthier relationship choices.

In conclusion, the emotional challenges faced by children of divorce are diverse and multifaceted. As educators, it is our responsibility to recognize and address these challenges, providing the necessary support and resources to help children build resilience and navigate the complex emotional landscape of divorce. By doing so, we can positively impact their overall well-being, academic performance, and future relationships.

Promoting Emotional Resilience in Children through Divorce

Divorce is a challenging and often traumatic experience for children. As educators, it is crucial for us to understand the emotional impact of divorce on children and find ways to promote their emotional resilience during this difficult time. By providing the right support and guidance, we can help children navigate their emotions, develop coping strategies, and build the resilience needed to thrive in the face of adversity.

One of the first steps in promoting emotional resilience in children through divorce is creating a safe and supportive environment. By fostering an atmosphere of trust and open communication, we can encourage children to express their feelings and concerns. This can be done through regular check-ins, one-on-one conversations, or even group discussions where children can share their experiences and support one another.

Another important aspect is helping children understand and manage their emotions. This can be achieved through age-appropriate activities such as journaling, art therapy, or mindfulness exercises. These activities not only allow children to express their emotions but also teach them valuable skills for regulating their emotions and reducing stress.

Additionally, it is crucial to provide children with accurate information about divorce and its effects. By explaining the changes that are occurring in their family in an age-appropriate manner, we can alleviate their fears and help them make sense of the situation. It is important to emphasize that the divorce is not their fault and that they are still loved and supported by both parents.

Furthermore, educators can play a significant role in connecting children with additional support resources. This may include school counselors, therapists, or support groups specifically designed for children of divorced parents. By collaborating with these professionals, we can ensure that children receive the necessary emotional support and guidance they need to thrive.

Lastly, promoting emotional resilience in children through divorce also involves fostering a sense of belonging and community. By encouraging positive social interactions, teamwork, and empathy within the classroom, we can help children develop strong social skills and build healthy relationships with their peers. This can have a long-term positive impact on their overall well-being and future romantic relationships.

In conclusion, promoting emotional resilience in children through divorce is crucial for their well-being and future success. As educators, we have the unique opportunity to provide the necessary support and guidance that can help children navigate the emotional challenges of divorce. By creating a safe and supportive environment, helping children understand and manage their emotions, providing accurate information, connecting them with support resources, and fostering a sense of belonging and community, we can empower children to develop the resilience needed to thrive in the face of adversity.

Effective Communication and Emotional Support for Children

In the midst of a divorce, children often face a plethora of emotional challenges that can have long-lasting effects on their well-being and development. As educators, it is crucial for us to understand the importance of effective communication and emotional support in helping children navigate through these difficult times.

One of the most significant effects of divorce on children is the disruption it causes to their daily routines and stability. This disruption can lead to feelings of confusion, anxiety, and sadness. To mitigate these emotions, it is essential to maintain open lines of communication with the children. Encourage them to express their thoughts and emotions freely, while assuring them that their feelings are valid and that they are not alone in this experience.

Listening attentively and empathetically is key to effective communication with children going through a divorce. Allow them to share their concerns, fears, and hopes without judgment. By actively listening, educators can validate their emotions and provide a safe space for them to process their feelings.

In addition to communication, emotional support plays a vital role in helping children cope with the psychological impact of divorce. As educators, we can offer emotional support by fostering a nurturing and inclusive classroom environment. This can be achieved by creating opportunities for students to engage in activities that promote self-expression and emotional resilience. For instance, integrating art therapy, journaling, or group discussions into the curriculum can provide children with a healthy outlet to express their emotions.

Furthermore, it is crucial to foster a sense of belonging and community within the classroom. Encourage peer support and collaboration, as this can help children develop positive social relationships and build resilience. Additionally, consider implementing mindfulness and relaxation techniques to help children manage stress and anxiety effectively.

By providing effective communication and emotional support, educators can play a significant role in mitigating the long-term effects of divorce on children. Academic performance can improve when children feel understood and supported emotionally. Furthermore, children's self-esteem and self-confidence can be positively influenced when they are encouraged to express their emotions and are provided with a safe and nurturing environment.

Ultimately, the impact of divorce on children's relationships, future romantic relationships, behavior, discipline, attachment styles, and mental health can be significantly influenced by the communication and emotional support they receive during this challenging time. As educators, we have the opportunity to make a lasting difference in the lives of these children by prioritizing effective communication and providing the emotional support they need to thrive.

Counseling and Therapy Options for Children's Emotional Well-being

One of the most challenging aspects of divorce is its impact on children's emotional well-being. As educators, it is essential to understand the various counseling and therapy options available to support children during this difficult time. By providing the necessary resources and guidance, we can help children build resilience and navigate the emotional challenges associated with divorce.

One effective counseling option for children is individual therapy. This type of therapy provides a safe space for children to express their feelings, fears, and concerns about the divorce. A trained therapist can help children develop coping strategies and build resilience, enabling them to navigate the emotional rollercoaster that often accompanies divorce. Individual therapy can also address any specific issues that may arise, such as anxiety, depression, or behavioral problems.

Group therapy is another valuable option for children experiencing the effects of divorce. In a group setting, children can connect with others who are going through similar experiences, providing a sense of support and understanding. Group therapy allows children to share their feelings, learn from one another, and develop important social skills. It can also help reduce feelings of isolation and provide a sense of belonging during a challenging time.

Family therapy is an essential component of supporting children's emotional well-being during a divorce. This type of therapy involves the entire family and provides a space for open communication and understanding. Family therapy can help parents and children navigate the changes and challenges associated with divorce, develop effective co-parenting strategies, and maintain healthy relationships. It also allows children to express their emotions and concerns while fostering a supportive and collaborative environment.

In addition to traditional therapy options, alternative approaches such as art therapy, play therapy, and mindfulness-based interventions can also be beneficial for children. These modalities provide creative outlets for self-expression and can help children process their emotions in a non-verbal and interactive way.

As educators, it is crucial to collaborate with mental health professionals to ensure children's emotional well-being is prioritized during and after a divorce. By recognizing the importance of counseling and therapy options, we can support children in building resilience, enhancing their self-esteem and self-confidence, and minimizing the long-term effects of divorce on their relationships, academic performance, emotional well-being, social development, mental health, attachment styles, behavior, discipline, and future romantic relationships.

Creating a Healthy Emotional Environment for Children of Divorce

Divorce can have a significant impact on children's emotional well-being and overall development. As educators, it is crucial for us to understand the effects of divorce on children and create a healthy emotional environment to support their resilience. By providing the right support, we can help children navigate through the challenges they may face and foster their self-esteem and self-confidence.

Firstly, it is important to acknowledge and validate the feelings of children whose parents are going through a divorce. Children may experience a range of emotions such as anger, sadness, confusion, and guilt. Creating a safe space where children can express their emotions without judgment is essential. Encourage them to share their feelings through various means like artwork, journaling, or group discussions.

Additionally, helping children maintain a sense of routine and stability can greatly contribute to their emotional well-being. Divorce often disrupts children's daily lives, so establishing consistent routines at school can provide them with a sense of security and predictability.

Consistency can also help children feel more in control of their lives during a time when they may feel a lack of control.

Furthermore, fostering open communication between children, parents, and educators is essential. Encourage parents to share information about the divorce and any changes in the child's life that may impact their behavior or emotions. Regular check-ins with children can help educators identify any signs of distress or changes in behavior that may require additional support.

Incorporating social-emotional learning (SEL) into the curriculum can also be beneficial. Teach children skills such as empathy, self-regulation, and problem-solving, which can help them cope with the challenges they may face due to their parents' divorce. SEL programs can provide children with the tools they need to navigate their emotions and build healthy relationships.

Lastly, collaborating with other professionals, such as school counselors or therapists, can offer additional support for children of divorce. These professionals can provide individual or group counseling sessions, allowing children to express their emotions and receive guidance on how to cope with their parents' divorce.

By creating a healthy emotional environment for children of divorce, educators can help mitigate the negative effects of divorce on their self-esteem, self-confidence, and overall development. It is through our understanding, empathy, and support that we can empower these children to build resilience and thrive academically, socially, and emotionally both during and after their parents' divorce.

Chapter 6: Divorce and Its Effect on Children's Self-esteem and Self-confidence

Understanding the Relationship between Divorce and Self-esteem

Divorce is a complex and emotionally challenging experience for children, and it can have a profound impact on their self-esteem and self-confidence. As educators, it is crucial to have a deep understanding of this relationship in order to provide the necessary support and guidance to children who have gone through a divorce.

One of the most significant effects of divorce on children's self-esteem is a feeling of rejection or abandonment. Children may blame themselves for their parents' separation, leading to a negative self-perception and a decline in self-esteem. As educators, it is essential to create a safe and nurturing environment where children can express their emotions and work through these feelings of self-doubt.

The psychological impact of divorce on children can also manifest in various ways, such as anxiety, depression, or behavioral problems. These emotional struggles can further contribute to a decline in self-esteem. By recognizing the signs of psychological distress, educators can offer the necessary support and connect children with appropriate resources, such as counseling services or support groups.

The long-term effects of divorce on children's relationships can also influence their self-esteem. Growing up in a divorced family may affect their ability to trust and form secure attachments with others. This can lead to a lack of self-confidence in building and maintaining healthy relationships. Educators can play a vital role in promoting positive social interactions within the classroom, teaching children empathy, and providing opportunities for building healthy relationships with peers.

Academic performance can also be impacted by divorce, which can further affect children's self-esteem. The stress and emotional turmoil associated with divorce can lead to difficulties in concentrating, decreased motivation, and a decline in academic achievement. By offering additional support and understanding, educators can help children overcome these challenges and regain their self-confidence in the academic setting.

It is important to note that not all children will experience the same effects of divorce on their self-esteem. Factors such as the age of the child, the level of conflict between parents, and the presence of a supportive network can influence the extent to which self-esteem is affected. As educators, it is crucial to be mindful of these individual differences and provide personalized support to each child.

In conclusion, divorce can have a significant impact on children's self-esteem and self-confidence. As educators, it is our responsibility to understand this relationship and provide the necessary support to help children navigate the challenges of divorce. By creating a nurturing and inclusive environment, offering emotional support, and promoting healthy relationships, we can help children build resilience and develop a positive self-image despite the challenges they may face.

Boosting Self-esteem and Self-confidence in Children of Divorce

Introduction:

Divorce can have a profound impact on children's self-esteem and self-confidence. As educators, it is crucial that we understand the unique challenges these children face and provide strategies to help them develop a strong sense of self-worth and resilience. In this subchapter, we will explore practical techniques to boost self-esteem and self-confidence in children of divorce, enabling them to navigate the challenges they may encounter.

1. Creating a Supportive Environment:

Educators play a vital role in creating a safe and supportive environment for children of divorce. By fostering a climate of acceptance, empathy, and understanding, we can help these children feel valued and heard. Encourage open communication, provide opportunities for expression, and ensure a non-judgmental atmosphere in the classroom.

2. Encouraging Positive Self-Image:

Help children of divorce develop a positive self-image by highlighting their strengths and accomplishments. Recognize their unique talents and abilities, and encourage them to set achievable goals. Celebrate their successes, no matter how small, to reinforce their self-worth and boost their confidence.

3. Building Resilience:

Resilience is crucial for children of divorce to navigate the emotional challenges they may face. Teach them coping skills, such as problem-solving strategies and stress management techniques. Encourage them to develop a growth mindset, emphasizing the importance of perseverance, adaptability, and learning from setbacks.

4. Fostering Healthy Relationships:

Positive relationships with peers and adults can significantly impact a child's self-esteem and self-confidence. Encourage cooperative learning activities, group projects, and team-building exercises to foster healthy relationships among classmates. Establish strong teacher-student relationships, providing guidance and support when needed.

5. Providing Counseling and Support Services:

Collaborate with school counselors and other professionals to provide counseling and support services to children of divorce. These services can help them process their emotions, develop coping strategies, and build resilience. By involving external resources, we can offer comprehensive support tailored to their needs.

Conclusion:

Boosting self-esteem and self-confidence in children of divorce is crucial for their overall well-being and future success. As educators, we have the power to create a nurturing environment that fosters resilience and growth. By implementing the strategies outlined in this subchapter, we can positively impact these children, helping them develop a strong sense of self-worth and confidence to navigate the challenges of divorce and thrive in all aspects of their lives.

Encouraging Positive Self-image and Identity Formation

In the midst of the challenges that children of divorce face, one crucial aspect that educators must prioritize is encouraging a positive self-image and supporting healthy identity formation. Divorce can have a profound impact on children's self-esteem and self-confidence, but with the right guidance, they can develop resilience and a strong sense of self.

One effective strategy is to create a safe and inclusive classroom environment where all students feel valued and respected. This can be achieved by promoting open discussions about emotions, family dynamics, and personal experiences related to divorce. By normalizing these conversations, educators can help children feel less alone and more understood, ultimately fostering positive self-image.

Furthermore, incorporating activities that encourage self-reflection and self-expression can be highly beneficial. For instance, journaling exercises can provide children with a private space to process their emotions and thoughts about their parents' divorce. Artistic outlets, such as drawing or painting, can also serve as a therapeutic means of self-expression, allowing children to explore their feelings in a creative and nonverbal way.

It is crucial for educators to be mindful of their language and interactions with students from divorced families. Avoiding stigmatizing language and assumptions about children's behavior or academic performance is essential. Instead, focusing on their strengths and abilities can help boost their self-esteem. Providing specific praise and recognition for their achievements, both inside and outside the classroom, can contribute to a positive self-image and foster a sense of accomplishment.

In addition to creating a supportive classroom environment, educators should collaborate with parents and other professionals to ensure a holistic approach to children's well-being. This may involve referring children to counseling services or support groups where they can receive specialized assistance in navigating the challenges of divorce.

By promoting positive self-image and identity formation, educators can equip children with the tools they need to thrive despite the impact of divorce. Through fostering resilience and self-confidence, children can develop a strong sense of self and build healthy relationships in the future. Remember, every child possesses unique strengths and potential, and it is our responsibility as educators to help them realize and embrace their true selves.

Addressing Self-esteem Issues in School Settings

In the aftermath of a divorce, children often experience a range of emotions that can impact their self-esteem and self-confidence. As educators, it is crucial for us to understand the effects of divorce on children and provide them with the support they need to address these self-esteem issues in school settings.

Research has shown that divorce can have a significant psychological impact on children. They may feel a sense of loss, confusion, and instability, leading to lower self-esteem and self-confidence. These feelings can manifest in various ways, such as decreased academic performance, emotional distress, and difficulties in social interactions.

One way to address self-esteem issues in school settings is to create a supportive and empathetic environment. Teachers can play a vital role in validating the children's feelings and providing them with a safe space to express themselves. By fostering open communication and showing understanding, educators can help children feel heard and valued.

Another important aspect is to promote a sense of belonging and inclusion within the classroom. Divorce can often disrupt a child's social development, making it crucial for educators to create opportunities for peer interaction and collaboration. Group projects, cooperative learning activities, and class discussions can all contribute to building positive relationships and boosting self-esteem.

Academic performance can be significantly affected by divorce, as children may struggle to concentrate or feel motivated. Educators can address these challenges by providing additional academic support, such as tutoring or individualized learning plans. By recognizing and reinforcing their strengths and achievements, teachers can help boost children's self-confidence and belief in their abilities.

Furthermore, it is essential to collaborate with school counselors and mental health professionals to identify children who may need additional support. Counseling sessions or support groups can provide children with a safe space to discuss their emotions and develop coping strategies. By addressing their emotional well-being, we can help improve their self-esteem and overall mental health.

Lastly, educators should also consider the long-term effects of divorce on children's relationships and future romantic relationships. By promoting healthy relationship skills, such as communication, empathy, and conflict resolution, we can empower children to build and maintain positive relationships throughout their lives.

In conclusion, divorce can have a profound impact on children's self-esteem and self-confidence. As educators, we have a unique opportunity to address these issues in school settings. By creating a supportive environment, promoting a sense of belonging, providing academic support, collaborating with mental health professionals, and fostering healthy relationship skills, we can help children navigate the challenges of divorce and build resilience for their future.

Fostering Resilience and Self-assurance in Children of Divorce

Introduction:

Children of divorce often face unique challenges that can affect their self-esteem and self-confidence. As educators, it is essential to understand the impact of divorce on children's emotional well-being and their long-term development. This subchapter will explore strategies for fostering resilience and self-assurance in children of divorce, with a focus on their academic performance, social development, and future relationships.

1. The Effects of A Divorce on The Children:

Divorce can have a profound impact on children, leading to feelings of insecurity, confusion, and a loss of stability. Educators should be aware of these effects and provide a supportive environment that helps children navigate through these challenges.

2. The Psychological Impact of Divorce on Children:

Divorce can cause psychological distress in children, including anxiety and depression. Educators can play a crucial role in promoting positive mental health by offering counseling services, encouraging open communication, and fostering a sense of belonging.

3. Academic Performance and Divorce: How it Affects Children's Education:

Divorce can negatively impact children's academic performance due to increased stress and disrupted routines. Educators can support children by creating a structured learning environment, providing individualized attention, and collaborating with parents to address any academic challenges.

4. Divorce and Its Impact on Children's Emotional Well-being:

Children of divorce may experience emotional difficulties, such as anger, sadness, or guilt. Educators can help by promoting emotional intelligence, teaching coping strategies, and providing a safe space for children to express their feelings.

5. Divorce and Its Effect on Children's Self-esteem and Self-confidence:

Divorce can shake children's self-esteem and self-confidence, leading to feelings of inadequacy and self-doubt. Educators can boost self-esteem by recognizing children's strengths, providing opportunities for success, and fostering a positive and inclusive classroom environment.

6. Divorce and Its Influence on Children's Social Development:

Divorce can impact children's social development, making them more prone to social withdrawal or difficulty forming relationships. Educators can facilitate social skills development through group activities, cooperative learning, and promoting empathy and inclusivity.

7. Divorce and Its Impact on Children's Mental Health:

Divorce can increase the risk of mental health issues in children, such as anxiety disorders or behavioral problems. Educators can collaborate with mental health professionals, implement trauma-informed practices, and provide resources for additional support.

8. Divorce and Its Effect on Children's Attachment Styles:

Divorce can influence children's attachment styles, affecting their ability to form healthy relationships in the future. Educators can promote secure attachments by nurturing a supportive and caring environment, modeling positive relationships, and encouraging healthy communication.

9. Divorce and Its Consequences on Children's Behavior and Discipline:

Children of divorce may exhibit challenging behaviors and difficulties with discipline. Educators can implement consistent and fair discipline strategies, provide clear expectations, and offer guidance on conflict resolution.

10. Divorce and Its Influence on Children's Future Romantic Relationships:

Divorce can shape children's beliefs and expectations about relationships, potentially impacting their future romantic relationships. Educators can promote healthy relationship skills through relationship education programs, teaching empathy, and fostering a positive attitude towards love and commitment.

Conclusion:

By understanding the unique challenges faced by children of divorce and implementing strategies to foster resilience and self-assurance, educators can play a vital role in supporting their emotional well-being, academic success, and future relationships. Creating a nurturing, inclusive, and supportive environment is crucial for helping children of divorce thrive despite the challenges they may face.

Chapter 7: Divorce and Its Influence on Children's Social Development

Social Challenges Faced by Children of Divorce

Divorce is a complex and challenging experience for children, and it often leads to various social challenges that can impact their overall well-being. As educators, it is crucial for us to understand these challenges and provide the necessary support to help children navigate through them.

One of the significant social challenges faced by children of divorce is the disruption in their social networks. Divorce often results in changes in living arrangements, which can mean moving to a new neighborhood or school. This transition can be difficult for children, as they may have to leave behind friends and familiar environments. As educators, we can play a vital role in helping them adjust by creating a welcoming and inclusive classroom environment, facilitating peer connections, and encouraging open communication.

Another social challenge that children of divorce commonly face is the stigma associated with their family situation. Society often places judgment and labels on children of divorce, which can negatively impact their self-esteem and self-confidence. Educators can counteract this by promoting empathy and understanding among students, fostering a supportive and inclusive school culture, and providing resources or programs that educate students about diverse family structures.

Divorce can also affect children's social development and their ability to form and maintain relationships. They may struggle with trust issues, fear of abandonment, or difficulty in managing conflict. As educators, we can help by promoting healthy relationship skills, teaching conflict resolution strategies, and providing a safe space for children to express their feelings and concerns.

Additionally, children of divorce may experience emotional difficulties that can affect their social interactions. They may exhibit signs of anxiety, depression, or anger, which can impact their ability to engage in social activities or make friends. It is essential for educators to be vigilant in recognizing these signs and providing appropriate support, such as counseling or access to mental health resources.

In conclusion, children of divorce face various social challenges that can impact their well-being and social development. Educators play a critical role in supporting these children by creating a nurturing and inclusive environment, promoting empathy and understanding, and providing resources and support to help them navigate through these challenges. By addressing the social challenges faced by children of divorce, we can contribute to building their resilience, self-esteem, and self-confidence, ultimately helping them thrive academically and in their future relationships.

Nurturing Healthy Social Skills and Friendships after Divorce

In the aftermath of a divorce, children often face significant challenges in their social development and the formation of healthy friendships. As educators, it is crucial for us to understand the various ways in which divorce can impact children's social skills, self-esteem, and self-confidence. By recognizing these effects, we can play a vital role in supporting their emotional well-being and fostering positive relationships.

Divorce can have a profound impact on children's social development. They may experience feelings of isolation, insecurity, and a loss of trust in others. These emotions can hinder their ability to form and maintain friendships. As educators, it is essential to create a safe and nurturing environment where children feel comfortable expressing their emotions and building connections with their peers.

One way to support children's social development is by encouraging open communication. Provide opportunities for children to share their feelings about the divorce, both with you and their peers. By fostering a non-judgmental and empathetic atmosphere, children can begin to process their emotions and develop healthier coping mechanisms.

Another crucial aspect is teaching children effective problem-solving and conflict resolution skills. Divorce often brings about increased tension and conflict within the family, which children may struggle to navigate. By teaching them strategies to manage conflicts constructively, such as active listening and compromise, we can empower them to build stronger friendships and handle challenging situations more effectively.

Furthermore, it is essential to promote resilience and self-esteem in children who have experienced divorce. Encourage them to participate in activities that align with their interests and strengths, providing opportunities for them to excel and gain confidence. Additionally, praising their efforts and achievements can boost their self-esteem and help them develop a positive self-image.

Lastly, as educators, we can also provide resources and support for parents navigating the challenges of post-divorce co-parenting. By working collaboratively with parents, we can ensure consistent messaging and support for the child's social development. Coordinating with parents to establish consistent rules and expectations can help children feel secure and provide a solid foundation for healthy friendships.

In conclusion, nurturing healthy social skills and friendships is crucial for children who have experienced divorce. By understanding the impacts of divorce on children's social development and implementing strategies to support their emotional well-being, educators can play a vital role in helping children build resilience and form positive relationships. By providing a safe and nurturing environment, teaching effective communication and problem-solving skills, promoting resilience and self-esteem, and collaborating with parents, we can help children overcome the challenges of divorce and thrive in their social interactions.

Addressing Social Stigma and Bullying

Social stigma and bullying are pervasive issues that can significantly impact children's self-esteem and self-confidence, especially in the context of divorce. Educators play a crucial role in addressing these challenges and creating a safe and inclusive environment for all students. This subchapter delves into the various ways in which educators can address social stigma and bullying in the lives of children affected by divorce.

1. Creating a supportive classroom environment: Educators should foster a classroom atmosphere that encourages empathy, respect, and understanding. By promoting open dialogue and teaching students about the diverse experiences of their peers, educators can help reduce stigma and foster a sense of inclusivity.

2. Promoting empathy and resilience: Educators can teach children the importance of empathy and resilience, helping them understand the impact of their words and actions on others. By emphasizing the value of kindness and respect, educators can empower children to stand up against bullying and support their peers.

3. Implementing anti-bullying policies and programs: Schools should establish clear and comprehensive anti-bullying policies that explicitly address the unique challenges faced by children of divorce. Educators

should also actively participate in anti-bullying programs, workshops, and training sessions to enhance their understanding of the issue and acquire effective strategies to prevent and address bullying incidents.

4. Encouraging open communication: Educators should create a safe space for children to express their feelings and concerns about divorce-related stigma and bullying. By fostering open communication, educators can identify and address any instances of bullying promptly, ensuring the emotional well-being of all students.

5. Collaborating with parents and guardians: Educators should maintain regular communication with parents and guardians to gain insight into the child's experiences at home and in the community. By working collaboratively, educators and parents can develop strategies to address social stigma and bullying, both inside and outside the classroom.

6. Providing support services: Schools should offer counseling services and support groups to children affected by divorce. These resources can help children develop coping mechanisms, build resilience, and navigate the challenges of social stigma and bullying effectively.

By addressing social stigma and bullying, educators can contribute to the overall well-being and academic success of children affected by divorce. Through their efforts, they can help children develop strong self-esteem, self-confidence, and healthy relationships, mitigating the long-term negative effects of divorce on their social development and future romantic relationships.

Positive Socialization Opportunities for Children of Divorce

Divorce can have a profound impact on children, affecting various aspects of their lives including their social development. As educators, it is crucial to understand the challenges these children face and provide them with positive socialization opportunities to help them thrive despite the circumstances. By creating a supportive and inclusive environment, educators can play a vital role in mitigating the negative effects of divorce on children's social development.

One important avenue for positive socialization is through peer interactions. Encouraging children of divorce to engage in group activities, such as sports teams, clubs, or community organizations, can help them build friendships and develop important social skills. By participating in these activities, children can form connections with peers who may share similar experiences, providing them with a sense of belonging and support.

Schools can also implement programs that promote empathy and emotional intelligence. Teaching children about empathy, understanding others' perspectives, and resolving conflicts peacefully can help them navigate the challenges of divorce more effectively. By fostering a culture of kindness and compassion, educators can create a safe space where children feel understood and valued.

Furthermore, collaboration between educators and parents is essential in supporting children's social development. Regular communication with parents can provide valuable insights into the child's needs and challenges, enabling educators to tailor their approach accordingly. Educators can also organize workshops or support groups for parents to address their concerns and provide guidance on helping their children cope with the social aspects of divorce.

In addition, it is important for educators to address any emotional or behavioral issues promptly. Children of divorce may experience a range of emotions, including sadness, anger, or resentment. By providing counseling services or access to mental health professionals, educators can offer children a supportive environment to express their feelings and develop healthy coping strategies.

Lastly, educators can incorporate activities that promote self-esteem and self-confidence into the curriculum. Engaging children in projects that encourage self-expression, such as art, music, or public speaking, can help boost their confidence and provide them with a sense of achievement. By recognizing and celebrating their strengths, educators can empower children to build a positive self-image despite the challenges they may face due to divorce.

In conclusion, educators have a unique opportunity to positively influence the social development of children of divorce. By providing inclusive environments, promoting empathy, fostering collaboration between parents and educators, addressing emotional and behavioral challenges, and promoting self-esteem, educators can help these children thrive and overcome the negative impact of divorce on their social development.

Supporting Healthy Social Development in the Classroom

In order to effectively support the healthy social development of children from divorced families, educators play a crucial role in creating a safe and inclusive classroom environment. By understanding the unique challenges these children face, educators can implement strategies that foster positive relationships and emotional well-being. This subchapter explores the importance of supporting healthy social development in the classroom and provides practical tips for educators.

Children from divorced families often experience a range of emotions, including sadness, anger, and confusion. These emotions can significantly impact their social interactions and relationships with peers. It is essential for educators to create a classroom environment that encourages open communication and empathy. By promoting a culture of respect and understanding, educators can help children feel safe and supported.

One effective strategy for supporting healthy social development is by incorporating social-emotional learning (SEL) into the curriculum. SEL activities teach children important skills such as empathy, self-awareness, and problem-solving. By integrating SEL into daily lessons, educators can help children develop the necessary emotional intelligence to navigate social situations effectively.

Furthermore, educators can foster healthy social development by promoting peer collaboration and positive relationships. Group projects and cooperative learning activities provide opportunities for children to work together, build trust, and develop teamwork skills. Educators can also encourage inclusive practices by promoting acceptance and appreciation of diversity within the classroom.

Additionally, educators should be vigilant in identifying signs of emotional distress in children from divorced families. These signs may include withdrawal, aggression, or changes in behavior. By being proactive and offering support, educators can help children navigate their emotions and build resilience.

Lastly, it is essential for educators to collaborate with parents and guardians. By maintaining open lines of communication, educators can gain valuable insights into each child's needs and provide consistent support. Regular parent-teacher meetings or progress reports can also serve as an opportunity to discuss any concerns or challenges that may arise.

By actively supporting healthy social development in the classroom, educators can make a significant impact on the lives of children from divorced families. By creating a nurturing and inclusive environment, promoting social-emotional learning, fostering positive relationships, and collaborating with parents, educators can help children navigate the challenges they may face and build a strong foundation for their future social interactions and relationships.

Chapter 8: Divorce and Its Impact on Children's Mental Health

Common Mental Health Issues in Children of Divorce

Divorce is a challenging experience for children, and it often leads to various mental health issues. As educators, it is crucial for us to understand these issues and provide the necessary support to help children cope with the psychological impact of divorce. This subchapter explores the common mental health issues faced by children of divorce and provides insights into how educators can address them.

One of the most prevalent mental health issues in children of divorce is anxiety. The uncertainty and changes that come with divorce can trigger feelings of fear and worry in children. They may become constantly worried about the future, their parents' relationship, and their own stability. As educators, creating a safe and supportive environment is crucial for alleviating anxiety in these children. By providing a stable and predictable routine, offering reassurance, and encouraging open communication, educators can help children feel more secure and reduce their anxiety levels.

Depression is another common mental health issue observed in children of divorce. The loss of the family unit and the emotional turmoil associated with divorce can lead to feelings of sadness, hopelessness, and low self-esteem. Educators can play a vital role in identifying signs of depression in children by observing changes in behavior, academic performance, and social interactions. By fostering a positive and nurturing environment, encouraging peer support, and involving school counselors, educators can help children combat depression and build their self-esteem.

Children of divorce may also struggle with behavioral issues such as aggression, disobedience, and impulsivity. The disruption in their family structure and the emotional stress they endure can impact their ability to regulate their emotions and behavior. Educators can assist these children by implementing consistent discipline strategies, teaching emotional regulation techniques, and providing opportunities for positive social interactions.

Furthermore, children of divorce may experience difficulties in forming and maintaining healthy relationships. The breakdown of their parents' marriage can influence their perception of relationships, leading to trust issues and fear of commitment. Educators can support these children by promoting healthy relationship skills, teaching empathy and communication, and providing guidance on building trust in relationships.

By understanding and addressing these common mental health issues, educators can play a vital role in helping children of divorce develop resilience and navigate the challenges they face. By creating a supportive and empathetic learning environment, educators can contribute to the long-term well-being and success of these children academically, socially, and emotionally.

Identifying Signs of Mental Health Distress in Children

Children who experience their parents' divorce often face various psychological challenges that can impact their mental health. As educators, it is crucial for us to be able to identify the signs of mental health distress in these children so that we can provide the necessary support and interventions. By being vigilant and observant, we can help mitigate the long-term effects of divorce on their emotional well-being and overall development.

One of the most common signs of mental health distress in children of divorce is a significant change in behavior. They may become withdrawn, exhibit increased aggression, or display sudden mood swings. These behavioral changes can be indicative of underlying emotional turmoil and should not be overlooked. Additionally, children may experience difficulty concentrating and a decline in academic performance. This decline may be linked to the emotional distress they are experiencing, as divorce can disrupt their routine and stability.

Another sign to watch out for is a decline in self-esteem and self-confidence. Children may start exhibiting negative self-talk, doubting their abilities, and having a pessimistic outlook on their future. They may also struggle with forming and maintaining healthy relationships with their peers, teachers, and even family members. This can be attributed to their fear of abandonment and a lack of trust resulting from the divorce.

Furthermore, children who are experiencing mental health distress may also exhibit physical symptoms such as headaches, stomachaches, or changes in appetite and sleep patterns. These physical manifestations can be a result of the stress and anxiety they are experiencing due to the divorce.

It is important for educators to maintain open lines of communication with the children and their families. By fostering a safe and supportive environment, children may feel more comfortable expressing their feelings and seeking help. Collaborating with school counselors and mental health professionals can also be instrumental in identifying and addressing mental health distress in children of divorce.

By recognizing the signs of mental health distress in children, educators can play a vital role in providing the necessary support and interventions. Through early identification and appropriate interventions, we can help mitigate the negative impact of divorce on children's mental health, self-esteem, and overall well-being. By promoting resilience and providing a nurturing environment, we can help them develop healthy coping mechanisms and lay the foundation for successful future relationships.

Accessing Mental Health Services for Children of Divorce

Divorce can have a profound impact on children's mental health, and it is crucial for educators to understand how this can affect their students. Many children of divorce experience heightened levels of stress, anxiety, and depression, making it essential for them to have access to mental health services. In this subchapter, we will explore the importance of accessing these services for children of divorce and provide educators with practical strategies to support their students.

Children of divorce often face unique challenges that can affect their overall well-being. They may struggle with feelings of loss, confusion, and guilt, which can manifest in various ways, such as behavioral issues, difficulty concentrating, or a decline in academic performance. Recognizing these signs and understanding the underlying mental health needs of these children is the first step in providing appropriate support.

Educators play a crucial role in identifying children who may require mental health services. By creating a safe and trusting environment, educators can encourage open communication and provide opportunities for children to express their emotions. It is important to be observant and look for any significant changes in behavior or mood that may indicate a need for additional support.

Once a child's mental health needs are identified, educators can help facilitate access to appropriate services. Collaborating with school counselors, psychologists, and social workers can ensure that children receive the necessary support. These professionals can offer individual or group therapy, counseling sessions, or referrals to external mental health providers if needed.

Furthermore, educators can advocate for the inclusion of mental health services within the school system. By raising awareness about the impact of divorce on children's mental health, educators can help secure funding and resources to establish or expand mental health programs within the school setting. This would provide children with easier access to the support they need, reducing barriers such as cost or transportation.

In conclusion, accessing mental health services is crucial for children of divorce to navigate the emotional challenges they may face. Educators have a unique opportunity to support these children by identifying their needs, facilitating access to services, and advocating for the inclusion of mental health programs within the school system. By prioritizing the mental well-being of children of divorce, educators can contribute to their resilience, self-esteem, and overall success within the educational setting and beyond.

Promoting Mental Wellness and Resilience in Children

As educators, it is crucial for us to understand the impact of divorce on children's mental wellness and resilience. Divorce can have significant effects on children's emotional well-being, self-esteem, and self-confidence. However, there are ways we can support and promote their mental wellness during this challenging time.

One of the key aspects to consider is the psychological impact of divorce on children. It is important to create a safe and supportive environment where children feel comfortable expressing their emotions and concerns. Encourage open communication and provide opportunities for them to share their feelings about the divorce. By validating their emotions, we can help them develop a sense of self-worth and resilience.

Another area to focus on is the long-term effects of divorce on children's relationships. Divorce can impact their ability to form healthy relationships in the future. As educators, we can help by teaching them essential social skills, such as effective communication, conflict resolution, and empathy. These skills will not only benefit them in their current relationships but also prepare them for successful future romantic relationships.

Academic performance is another area that can be affected by divorce. Children may experience difficulties concentrating, completing assignments, or participating in class. It is essential to provide additional support and resources to help them navigate these challenges. Collaborate with parents and other professionals to create an individualized plan that addresses their academic needs while considering their emotional well-being.

Furthermore, divorce can influence children's attachment styles and their ability to form secure relationships. Educators can play a crucial role in promoting secure attachments by providing a nurturing and consistent environment. Be mindful of the child's need for stability and predictability, and offer opportunities for them to form positive relationships with peers and adults.

Lastly, it is important to address the consequences of divorce on children's behavior and discipline. Divorce can lead to behavioral changes, such as acting out or withdrawal. By implementing positive behavior management strategies and providing emotional support, we can help children develop appropriate coping mechanisms and resilience.

In conclusion, promoting mental wellness and resilience in children affected by divorce is a crucial task for educators. By understanding the psychological impact of divorce, focusing on long-term effects, supporting academic performance, fostering secure attachments, addressing behavior and discipline, and guiding them towards healthy relationships, we can empower children to navigate the challenges they face and thrive both academically and emotionally.

Collaborating with Mental Health Professionals to Support Children

Divorce can have a significant impact on children's mental health and well-being. As educators, it is crucial for us to recognize the importance of collaborating with mental health professionals to provide the necessary support for children experiencing the effects of divorce.

One of the primary effects of divorce on children is the psychological impact it can have. Children may experience feelings of sadness, confusion, anger, and anxiety as their family dynamics change. By working closely with mental health professionals, educators can gain valuable insights into the emotional needs of these children and develop strategies to address them effectively.

Moreover, divorce can have long-term effects on children's relationships. They may struggle with trust issues, have difficulty forming and maintaining healthy relationships, and develop negative attachment styles. Mental health professionals can offer guidance on how to help children navigate these challenges and develop healthy relationship skills.

Academic performance is another area that can be significantly affected by divorce. Children may experience a decline in their academic performance due to increased stress, emotional turmoil, or disrupted routines. Mental health professionals can assist educators in creating a supportive environment, implementing coping mechanisms, and identifying any additional educational needs that may arise.

The emotional well-being of children should also be a top priority. Divorce can lead to feelings of low self-esteem and self-confidence. Collaborating with mental health professionals can enable educators to implement strategies that promote emotional resilience and self-empowerment, helping children rebuild their self-esteem and confidence.

Social development is another critical aspect that can be impacted by divorce. Children may struggle with forming friendships, engaging in social activities, or displaying appropriate social skills. Mental health professionals can provide educators with tools to support children in developing healthy social connections and fostering a sense of belonging.

In addition, divorce can have a profound impact on children's mental health. They may experience symptoms of anxiety, depression, or even trauma. By working alongside mental health professionals, educators can identify signs of distress, offer appropriate support, and refer children to the necessary resources for professional intervention.

Understanding the effect of divorce on children's attachment styles is also essential. Children may develop insecure attachment styles, which can affect their future relationships. Mental health professionals can guide educators in creating a nurturing and secure environment that supports healthy attachment and helps children develop secure relationship patterns.

Lastly, divorce can influence children's behavior and discipline. They may exhibit challenging behaviors or struggle with self-regulation. Mental health professionals can provide educators with strategies to address these behaviors effectively, promote positive discipline techniques, and create a supportive and structured environment.

By collaborating with mental health professionals, educators can play a crucial role in supporting children through the challenges of divorce. Together, we can help children build resilience, develop healthy coping mechanisms, and thrive academically, emotionally, and socially.

Chapter 9: Divorce and Its Effect on Children's Attachment Styles

Understanding Attachment Theory and Divorce

Attachment theory provides valuable insights into how divorce affects children's emotional well-being, self-esteem, and future relationships. As educators, it is crucial to have a deep understanding of this theory in order to support children going through divorce effectively.

Attachment theory, developed by John Bowlby, emphasizes the importance of the parent-child relationship in a child's development. It suggests that children form an emotional bond with their primary caregiver, usually the mother, during their early years. This bond, known as the secure attachment, provides a sense of security and forms the foundation for healthy emotional and social development.

When divorce occurs, it disrupts the secure attachment between the child and the primary caregiver. This disruption can lead to various psychological impacts on children. They may experience feelings of abandonment, fear, and confusion, which can negatively affect their self-esteem and self-confidence. It is essential for educators to be aware of these potential impacts and provide a supportive and nurturing environment for children to cope with these emotions.

Furthermore, research has shown that the long-term effects of divorce on children's relationships can be significant. Children who experience divorce may have difficulty forming secure attachments in future romantic relationships. They may struggle with trust issues, fear of abandonment, and difficulty forming deep emotional connections. Educators can play a vital role in helping children develop healthy relationship skills by providing guidance and teaching them about healthy communication, empathy, and emotional regulation.

Academic performance can also be affected by divorce. Children may experience difficulties concentrating in school, have lower grades, and struggle with motivation. Educators should be sensitive to these challenges and provide extra support and understanding to help children overcome academic obstacles.

In terms of social development, divorce can impact children's ability to form and maintain friendships. They may feel isolated or have difficulty trusting others. Educators can help by fostering a supportive and inclusive classroom environment that encourages positive social interactions and provides opportunities for children to build healthy relationships with their peers.

Overall, understanding attachment theory and its implications for children going through divorce is crucial for educators. By being knowledgeable about the effects of divorce on children's self-esteem, self-confidence, relationships, academic performance, and emotional well-being, educators can provide the necessary support and guidance to help children build resilience and navigate through this challenging period in their lives.

Different Attachment Outcomes in Children of Divorce

When parents go through a divorce, it can have a significant impact on their children's attachment styles and relationships. Attachment theory suggests that the quality of early relationships with caregivers sets the stage for how individuals form and maintain relationships throughout their lives. In the context of divorce, children may experience various attachment outcomes, each with its own implications for their emotional well-being, self-esteem, and future relationships.

One possible attachment outcome is insecure attachment. Children who have experienced the disruption and loss associated with divorce may exhibit insecure attachment patterns. These children may struggle with trust, fear abandonment, and have difficulty forming close relationships. Educators should be aware of these challenges and provide a nurturing and supportive environment to help these children feel secure and develop healthy attachment styles.

On the other hand, some children may develop secure attachment despite the divorce. These children have experienced consistent and responsive caregiving, even in the midst of their parents' separation. They are more likely to have positive self-esteem, confidence, and healthy relationship patterns. Educators can play a vital role in reinforcing these secure attachments by providing a safe and supportive space for children to express their feelings and offering guidance on building and maintaining healthy relationships.

Another attachment outcome that can be observed in children of divorce is disorganized attachment. This type of attachment is characterized by contradictory behaviors, confusion, and fear. Children with disorganized attachment may struggle with emotional regulation, exhibit aggressive or withdrawn behavior, and have difficulty forming lasting relationships. Educators should be attuned to these signs and work collaboratively with parents, counselors, and other professionals to provide the necessary support and interventions to help these children develop more secure attachment patterns.

It is crucial for educators to understand the different attachment outcomes in children of divorce and their implications for various aspects of their lives. By recognizing the challenges these children may face in forming and maintaining relationships, educators can implement strategies that promote resilience, self-esteem, and self-confidence. Additionally, educators can provide resources and support to help children navigate the emotional and social impact of divorce, ultimately fostering healthy development and positive future relationships.

In conclusion, divorce can have significant effects on children's attachment styles and relationships. Educators have a unique opportunity to support children of divorce by understanding the different attachment outcomes they may experience. By providing a nurturing and supportive environment, educators can help children develop secure attachments, overcome challenges associated with insecure or disorganized attachments, and ultimately thrive in their academic and personal lives.

Building Secure Attachments in Children after Divorce

Introduction:

Divorce can have a profound impact on children's emotional well-being and development. One crucial aspect affected by divorce is the formation of secure attachments between children and their caregivers. As educators, it is essential to understand the significance of building secure attachments in children after divorce and how it can positively influence various aspects of their lives.

The Importance of Secure Attachments:

Secure attachments lay the foundation for healthy emotional development, social relationships, and academic success. Children who have secure attachments feel safe, supported, and loved. They are more likely to develop resilience, self-esteem, and self-confidence, even in the face of adversity.

Factors Influencing Attachment Styles:

Divorce can disrupt the formation of secure attachments due to various factors. These include parental conflict, changes in living arrangements, and potential emotional neglect. As educators, we must be aware of these factors to provide appropriate support and guidance to children navigating through this challenging period.

Promoting Secure Attachments:

1. Encourage open communication: Create a safe and nurturing environment where children feel comfortable expressing their feelings and concerns. Encourage them to discuss their experiences and listen attentively without judgment.

2. Foster positive relationships: Strengthen the bond between children and their caregivers by promoting positive interactions and shared experiences. Encourage parents to spend quality time with their children and engage in activities that promote connection and emotional closeness.

3. Provide support and consistency: Consistency in routines and expectations can help children feel secure. Collaborate with parents to establish consistent rules and boundaries at home and school, ensuring a stable and predictable environment for the child.

4. Empower children: Help children develop a sense of autonomy and independence by providing opportunities for decision-making and problem-solving. Encourage their participation in extracurricular activities or hobbies that promote self-expression and personal growth.

5. Collaborate with parents and professionals: Maintain open lines of communication with parents and collaborate with mental health professionals when necessary. This collaborative approach can ensure that children receive the necessary support to cope with the emotional challenges of divorce.

Conclusion:

Building secure attachments in children after divorce is crucial for their overall well-being and development. As educators, we have a unique opportunity to provide a supportive and nurturing environment for children, helping them overcome the challenges associated with divorce. By promoting open communication, fostering positive relationships, providing support and consistency, empowering children, and collaborating with parents and professionals, we can contribute to the development of resilient and confident individuals who can form healthy relationships in the future.

Healing Attachment Wounds in Children of Divorce

Introduction:

Divorce can have a profound impact on children, affecting various aspects of their lives including their emotional well-being, academic performance, social development, and future relationships. One of the key areas that is often overlooked is the impact on children's attachment styles, which can have long-term effects on their ability to form healthy relationships. In this subchapter, we will explore the concept of attachment wounds in children of divorce and provide educators with strategies to support their healing process.

Understanding Attachment Wounds:

Attachment wounds refer to the emotional injuries experienced by children when their primary caregivers, typically their parents, are unable to provide a secure and nurturing environment during and after a divorce. These wounds can lead to insecure attachment styles, such as anxious or avoidant attachment, which can interfere with children's ability to trust and form healthy relationships.

Impact on Children's Relationships:

Children of divorce often struggle with forming and maintaining relationships due to their attachment wounds. They may exhibit behaviors such as fear of abandonment, difficulty expressing emotions, and challenges in establishing boundaries. Educators play a vital role in helping these children develop secure attachment styles and build resilience.

Strategies for Healing Attachment Wounds:

1. Creating a Safe and Supportive Environment: Educators can create a classroom environment that fosters trust and emotional safety. This can be achieved by establishing clear expectations, providing consistent support, and promoting open communication.

2. Implementing Trauma-Informed Practices: By incorporating trauma-informed practices into their teaching, educators can better understand the unique needs of children of divorce and respond sensitively. This includes recognizing triggers, offering coping strategies, and providing appropriate resources.

3. Encouraging Therapeutic Interventions: Educators can collaborate with mental health professionals to identify children who may benefit from therapy or counseling. These interventions can help children process their emotions, develop healthier attachment styles, and build resilience.

4. Promoting Social-Emotional Learning: Integrating social-emotional learning into the curriculum can help children develop self-awareness, empathy, and emotional regulation skills. This can support their healing process and enhance their ability to form positive relationships.

Conclusion:

Healing attachment wounds in children of divorce is a complex process that requires the collective effort of parents, educators, and mental health professionals. By understanding the impact of divorce on children's attachment styles and implementing strategies to support their healing, educators can play a crucial role in helping children build resilience, develop healthy relationships, and thrive academically, socially, and emotionally.

Promoting Healthy Attachment in the Classroom

In the aftermath of a divorce, children often experience a range of emotions and challenges that can impact their overall well-being and academic performance. As educators, it is crucial for us to understand the importance of promoting healthy attachment in the classroom to support these children in their healing process and to ensure their educational success. This subchapter aims to provide strategies and insights on how educators can foster healthy attachment in the classroom and mitigate the negative effects of divorce on children's self-esteem, self-confidence, and relationships.

One of the first steps in promoting healthy attachment is creating a safe and supportive classroom environment. This can be achieved by establishing clear expectations, maintaining consistent routines, and providing opportunities for open communication and emotional expression. By fostering a sense of security and trust, children are more likely to develop positive relationships with their peers and feel comfortable seeking help and support from their teachers.

Another important aspect is recognizing and addressing the unique needs of children affected by divorce. These children may require additional support and understanding during times of emotional distress. Educators can create a culture of empathy and compassion by implementing social-emotional learning programs and incorporating activities that encourage self-reflection and emotional regulation. By equipping children with the tools to understand and manage their emotions, educators can help them navigate the challenges associated with divorce more effectively.

Furthermore, it is crucial to involve parents and guardians in the process of promoting healthy attachment. Educators can establish regular communication channels with families, providing updates on the child's progress and offering resources for support. Collaborating with parents can help create a consistent and nurturing environment both at home and in the classroom, reinforcing the child's sense of stability and trust.

Finally, educators should prioritize building strong and positive relationships with each individual child. Taking the time to understand their unique strengths, interests, and challenges can help create a sense of belonging and foster a secure attachment. By providing personalized support and encouragement, educators can empower children affected by divorce to build resilience, enhance their self-esteem, and develop healthy attachment styles that will positively influence their future relationships.

Promoting healthy attachment in the classroom is not only vital for the academic success of children affected by divorce but also for their overall well-being and future relationships. By creating a safe and supportive environment, addressing their unique needs, involving parents, and building strong relationships, educators can play a crucial role in helping children navigate the challenges of divorce and build a foundation for a resilient and successful future.

Chapter 10: Divorce and Its Consequences on Children's Behavior and Discipline

Behavioral Changes and Challenges in Children after Divorce

Divorce is a life-altering event that can have a significant impact on children's behavior and overall well-being. As educators, it is crucial for us to understand these changes and challenges in order to support our students during this difficult time. In this subchapter, we will explore the various behavioral changes that children may exhibit after a divorce and the challenges they may face as a result.

One of the most common behavioral changes seen in children after a divorce is an increase in aggression and acting out. This can manifest in the form of tantrums, defiance, and even physical aggression towards peers or authority figures. These behaviors are often a result of the emotional turmoil and stress that children experience during and after a divorce.

In addition to aggression, children may also exhibit withdrawal and social isolation. They may become more reserved, reluctant to engage in social activities, and have difficulty forming or maintaining friendships. This can be attributed to feelings of insecurity, fear of rejection, and a lack of trust in others. As educators, it is important for us to create a supportive and inclusive environment where these children feel safe to express themselves and form connections with their peers.

Academically, children may experience a decline in their performance after a divorce. This can be attributed to a range of factors including decreased parental involvement, increased emotional distress, and disrupted routines. It is crucial for us as educators to provide additional support and resources to help these children stay on track academically and address any learning difficulties they may be facing.

Another challenge that children face after a divorce is a decrease in self-esteem and self-confidence. The breakdown of their parents' relationship can lead to feelings of guilt, shame, and a sense of unworthiness. It is essential for us to encourage and uplift these children, helping them rebuild their self-esteem and regain their confidence.

Furthermore, the long-term effects of divorce on children's relationships and future romantic relationships cannot be overlooked. Children who witness their parents' divorce may develop negative attitudes towards relationships, struggle with trust issues, and have difficulties forming intimate connections later in life. As educators, we can play a crucial role in promoting healthy relationship building skills and providing guidance on navigating emotional challenges.

In conclusion, divorce can have significant behavioral changes and challenges for children. As educators, it is our responsibility to understand these effects and provide the necessary support to help our students navigate through this difficult time. By creating a safe and supportive environment, addressing academic challenges, and promoting healthy relationship skills, we can help children build resilience and thrive despite the challenges they may face due to divorce.

Effective Discipline Strategies for Children of Divorce

Introduction:

Divorce can have a significant impact on children's emotional well-being, self-esteem, and self-confidence. As educators, it is crucial for us to understand the unique challenges that children of divorce face and provide them with effective discipline strategies to help them navigate through this difficult period. This subchapter explores various discipline strategies that can support children of divorce and promote their resilience.

1. Consistency and Structure:

Children of divorce often experience a sense of instability and uncertainty. Providing them with a consistent and structured environment can help them feel secure. Establish clear rules and expectations, and ensure that they are consistently applied both at home and in the school setting. This consistency will provide a sense of stability and security for the children.

2. Open Communication:

Encourage open communication with children of divorce. Create a safe space where they feel comfortable expressing their feelings and concerns. By actively listening and validating their experiences, educators can help children process their emotions and develop healthy coping mechanisms.

3. Collaboration with Parents:

Maintaining a strong partnership with parents is crucial when addressing discipline strategies for children of divorce. Regularly communicate with parents to gain insight into the specific challenges their child may be facing. Collaborate on disciplinary approaches that are consistent across home and school, ensuring that boundaries and expectations remain intact.

4. Positive Reinforcement:

Children of divorce may experience feelings of guilt or low self-esteem. Utilize positive reinforcement techniques to build their self-confidence and self-worth. Recognize and celebrate their achievements, no matter how small, to promote a positive sense of self.

5. Emotional Support:

Divorce can be emotionally challenging for children, impacting their behavior and discipline. Provide emotional support by offering counseling services or connecting them with support groups where they can share their experiences with peers who may be going through similar situations. This support can help them develop healthy coping mechanisms and improve their overall well-being.

Conclusion:

By implementing these effective discipline strategies, educators can help children of divorce build resilience, develop positive self-esteem, and enhance their self-confidence. Remember that each child's experience is unique, so it is essential to approach discipline strategies with empathy, understanding, and a genuine desire to support their emotional and academic growth. Together, we can provide children of divorce with the tools they need to thrive academically, socially, and emotionally, despite the challenges they may face.

Addressing Behavioral Issues in School Settings

When it comes to addressing behavioral issues in school settings, educators play a crucial role in supporting children who have experienced the effects of divorce. Divorce can have a significant impact on children's behavior, and understanding how to effectively address these issues is essential for their academic success and overall well-being.

One of the key effects of divorce on children is the psychological impact it can have. Many children may experience feelings of sadness, anger, confusion, or even guilt, which can manifest in their behavior at school. Educators need to be aware of these emotional challenges and provide a supportive environment where children feel safe to express their emotions.

Additionally, the long-term effects of divorce on children's relationships can also contribute to behavioral issues. Children may struggle with forming healthy relationships, both with their peers and authority figures. Educators can help by promoting positive social interactions, teaching conflict resolution skills, and providing opportunities for children to build healthy relationships with their peers.

Academic performance is another area that can be affected by divorce. Children may struggle to concentrate, experience a decline in grades, or show a lack of motivation. Educators can address these issues by implementing strategies to support academic success, such as providing extra academic support, offering counseling services, or creating a structured and nurturing classroom environment.

Divorce can also impact children's emotional well-being, self-esteem, and self-confidence. Educators can foster a positive and inclusive classroom environment that promotes a sense of belonging and encourages children to develop a healthy sense of self. By providing opportunities for success and recognizing their strengths, educators can help children rebuild their self-esteem and confidence.

Furthermore, divorce can influence children's social development and attachment styles. Some children may struggle with forming secure attachments or may exhibit clingy or avoidant behavior. Educators can support these children by providing a nurturing and consistent environment, promoting healthy attachment relationships, and teaching social-emotional skills.

Moreover, divorce can have consequences on children's behavior and discipline. Some children may act out, become withdrawn, or exhibit disruptive behavior in the classroom. Educators can address these issues by implementing positive behavior management strategies, providing individualized support, and collaborating with parents to develop consistent discipline strategies.

Lastly, divorce can also influence children's future romantic relationships. Educators can play a role in providing education and guidance on healthy relationships, promoting open communication, and teaching conflict resolution skills.

In conclusion, addressing behavioral issues in school settings for children affected by divorce requires a comprehensive approach. By understanding the effects of divorce on children's self-esteem, relationships, academic performance, and overall well-being, educators can provide the necessary support and create an environment where children can thrive academically and emotionally.

Collaborating with Parents to Encourage Positive Behavior

When it comes to divorce, children often experience a wide range of emotions and challenges that can impact their self-esteem, self-confidence, and overall well-being. As educators, we play a crucial role in supporting these children through their journey of healing and growth. One effective way to do this is by collaborating with parents to encourage positive behavior.

Parents are the primary influencers in a child's life, and their involvement in the educational process can make a significant difference in the child's overall development. By working together, educators and parents can create a supportive and nurturing environment that fosters resilience and helps children overcome the negative effects of divorce.

To collaborate effectively with parents, it is essential to establish open lines of communication. Regularly updating parents about their child's progress, behavior, and achievements can help them stay informed and involved. This can be done through parent-teacher conferences, progress reports, or even a simple email or phone call. By keeping parents in the loop, they can actively participate in addressing any behavioral issues that may arise due to divorce.

Additionally, educators can offer resources and support to parents to help them navigate the challenges their children may face. Providing information on counseling services, support groups, or recommended books can empower parents to seek the necessary help for their child's emotional well-being. By equipping parents with the tools they need, educators can ensure a holistic approach to supporting children through divorce.

Another important aspect of collaborating with parents is offering strategies for discipline and behavior management that are consistent both at home and at school. By aligning expectations and reinforcing positive behavior, children can experience stability and a sense of security in their daily lives. This consistency can greatly contribute to their self-esteem and self-confidence.

Furthermore, educators can engage parents in discussions about their child's academic performance and provide suggestions for supporting their education during and after a divorce. By offering guidance on creating a routine, setting realistic goals, and providing a nurturing environment for learning, parents can play an active role in promoting their child's academic success.

In conclusion, collaborating with parents is essential in helping children navigate the challenges of divorce and promoting their overall well-being. By establishing open lines of communication, offering resources and support, aligning discipline strategies, and involving parents in their child's education, educators can make a positive impact on the effects of divorce on children. Together, we can foster resilience, boost self-esteem, and ensure a brighter future for these children in their relationships, education, and overall development.

Teaching Coping Skills and Emotional Regulation Techniques

In the face of a divorce, children often experience a wide range of emotions and difficulties in managing their feelings. As educators, it is crucial for us to provide support and guidance to help children develop coping skills and emotional regulation techniques. By doing so, we can contribute to their overall resilience and well-being.

One effective way to teach coping skills is through the promotion of open communication. Encourage children to express their emotions and thoughts about the divorce in a safe and non-judgmental environment. By providing a listening ear, you can validate their feelings and help them process their emotions. It is important to remind children that their feelings are valid and that it is normal to experience a wide range of emotions during this challenging time.

Another valuable coping skill is the practice of self-care. Encourage children to engage in activities that promote a sense of well-being and relaxation. This could include exercise, hobbies, spending time with friends and family, or engaging in creative outlets such as art or music. By promoting self-care, children can learn to prioritize their own mental health and develop healthy ways of managing stress.

Teaching emotional regulation techniques is equally important. Help children identify their emotions and understand that all emotions are valid. Teach them strategies such as deep breathing exercises, mindfulness techniques, and positive self-talk to manage their emotions effectively. By practicing these techniques, children can learn to regulate their emotions in a healthy manner, reducing the risk of negative emotional outcomes.

Furthermore, teaching problem-solving skills can empower children to navigate the challenges that arise from a divorce. Encourage children to brainstorm solutions to their problems and consider the potential outcomes of each option. By fostering their problem-solving abilities, you can equip them with the skills to overcome obstacles and make sound decisions.

In conclusion, teaching coping skills and emotional regulation techniques to children experiencing divorce is vital for their resilience and well-being. As educators, we have the opportunity to provide support and guidance, helping children develop the necessary skills to navigate this challenging period in their lives. By promoting open communication, self-care, emotional regulation, and problem-solving skills, we can contribute to their long-term emotional and psychological growth.

Chapter 11: Divorce and Its Influence on Children's Future Romantic Relationships

Understanding the Link between Divorce and Romantic Relationships

Divorce is a significant life event that has a profound impact on children, particularly in relation to their future romantic relationships. It is crucial for educators to comprehend the link between divorce and romantic relationships in order to better support children who have experienced their parents' separation. This subchapter aims to shed light on this relationship and provide educators with valuable insights.

Research suggests that children of divorced parents may face challenges in their own romantic relationships. The effects of a divorce on children, such as decreased self-esteem, self-confidence, and emotional well-being, can manifest in their future romantic relationships. These children may struggle with trust issues, fear of abandonment, and difficulty forming secure attachments. Therefore, educators must be mindful of these potential challenges and provide appropriate support and guidance.

Furthermore, the psychological impact of divorce on children can have long-term effects on their relationships. Children who witnessed their parents' separation may develop negative beliefs about relationships and commitment. They may also struggle with effective communication, conflict resolution, and intimacy. Educators can play a crucial role in promoting healthy relationship skills by teaching students effective communication techniques, conflict resolution strategies, and providing them with tools to build trust and establish secure attachments.

Divorce can also affect children's academic performance and educational achievements. The stress and emotional turmoil caused by the divorce can hinder a child's ability to concentrate and excel academically. It is essential for educators to identify and support these children, providing them with additional resources and counseling services to help them cope and succeed in their educational endeavors.

Moreover, divorce has a significant impact on children's mental health, behavior, and discipline. Children of divorced parents may exhibit higher levels of anxiety, depression, and behavioral problems. Educators should be knowledgeable about the potential behavioral challenges that these children may face and implement appropriate disciplinary strategies that promote understanding, empathy, and emotional support.

Understanding the link between divorce and children's future romantic relationships is vital for educators. By recognizing the potential challenges and providing appropriate support, educators can help children build resilience and develop healthy relationship skills. By fostering a nurturing and empathetic learning environment, educators can contribute to the long-term well-being and success of children who have experienced divorce.

Impact of Divorce on Relationship Patterns in Adulthood

Divorce has a profound impact on children's lives, and this impact can extend well into adulthood, particularly in the realm of relationships. As educators, it is important for us to understand how divorce affects children's relationship patterns in adulthood, so that we can provide the necessary support and guidance to help them navigate these challenges.

One of the key effects of divorce on children's relationship patterns in adulthood is a higher likelihood of experiencing relationship difficulties. Research has consistently shown that individuals who come from divorced families are more likely to have unstable and short-lived relationships compared to those who come from intact families. These individuals may struggle with trust issues, fear of commitment, and difficulty in forming secure attachments with their partners.

Additionally, the psychological impact of divorce can manifest in various ways in adulthood. Children who have experienced divorce may have lower self-esteem and self-confidence, which can affect their ability to form and maintain healthy relationships. They may also exhibit higher levels of anxiety and depression, making it challenging for them to engage in meaningful connections with others.

The long-term effects of divorce on children's relationships can also be seen in their academic performance. Research has shown that children of divorce are more likely to experience academic difficulties, such as lower grades and decreased motivation. These struggles can further impact their self-esteem and confidence, making it harder for them to establish and maintain healthy relationships in adulthood.

Furthermore, divorce can have a significant impact on children's emotional well-being. Growing up in a divorced family can lead to feelings of insecurity and instability, which can make it harder for individuals to trust and open up in future relationships. They may also struggle with feelings of guilt and blame, which can further complicate their ability to form healthy connections with others.

Divorce can also influence children's social development. Those who have experienced divorce may have difficulty in developing and maintaining friendships. They may feel different or stigmatized compared to their peers from intact families, leading to feelings of isolation and loneliness. These challenges can persist into adulthood, making it harder for individuals to form meaningful and supportive relationships.

In conclusion, divorce has a significant impact on children's relationship patterns in adulthood. As educators, it is crucial for us to be aware of these effects and provide the necessary support and guidance to help children navigate these challenges. By understanding the long-term consequences of divorce on children's relationships, we can better equip them with the tools and resources to build healthy and fulfilling connections in their adult lives.

Nurturing Healthy Relationship Skills in Children of Divorce

Divorce can have a significant impact on children's overall well-being, including their ability to form and maintain healthy relationships. As educators, it is crucial for us to recognize the unique challenges that children of divorce face and to provide them with the necessary support and guidance to develop strong relationship skills. By nurturing these skills, we can help them build resilience and navigate future relationships successfully.

One of the first steps in nurturing healthy relationship skills in children of divorce is to create a safe and supportive environment within the school setting. This can be achieved by promoting open communication, empathy, and understanding. Encourage children to express their feelings and thoughts about their parents' divorce, while also providing them with the necessary tools to manage their emotions effectively.

Teaching children effective communication skills is another crucial aspect of nurturing healthy relationships. Provide them with opportunities to practice active listening, expressing themselves assertively, and resolving conflicts in a respectful manner. These skills will not only benefit their relationships with peers but also with family members and future romantic partners.

It is also important to address any misconceptions or negative beliefs that children may have developed about relationships as a result of their parents' divorce. Provide them with accurate information about healthy relationships, emphasizing the importance of trust, respect, and mutual support. Encourage them to challenge any negative assumptions they may have and guide them towards positive role models.

Furthermore, incorporating social-emotional learning programs into the curriculum can be highly beneficial for children of divorce. These programs can teach them essential skills such as empathy, emotional regulation, and problem-solving, which are crucial in building and maintaining healthy relationships.

Lastly, collaboration with parents is essential in nurturing healthy relationship skills in children of divorce. Offer resources and support to parents, such as workshops on co-parenting, effective communication, and conflict resolution. Encourage parents to maintain a positive co-parenting relationship, as children learn relationship skills by observing their parents' interactions.

By focusing on nurturing healthy relationship skills in children of divorce, educators can play a vital role in mitigating the negative long-term effects of divorce on their relationships. By providing them with the necessary support and guidance, we can empower these children to build resilience, develop strong relationship skills, and thrive in their future relationships.

Addressing Trust and Commitment Issues in Future Relationships

In the aftermath of a divorce, children often experience a wide range of emotions, including trust and commitment issues that can have a lasting impact on their future relationships. As educators, it is crucial for us to understand the effects of divorce on children's trust and commitment, and to provide them with the necessary tools and support to navigate these challenges.

Divorce can shatter a child's belief in the stability of relationships and make them question the trustworthiness of others. This can lead to difficulties in forming and maintaining relationships in the future. It is essential for educators to create a safe and supportive environment where children can openly express their feelings and fears about trust and commitment.

One effective strategy is to incorporate activities that promote trust-building and teamwork into the curriculum. Group projects and collaborative learning experiences can help children develop trust in their peers and build positive relationships. By fostering an atmosphere of trust and respect in the classroom, educators can help children rebuild their trust in others.

In addition to addressing trust issues, it is important to help children understand the concept of commitment and its role in relationships. Educators can introduce age-appropriate discussions and activities that emphasize the importance of commitment, loyalty, and reliability. Teaching children about the value of keeping promises and fulfilling responsibilities can help them develop a stronger sense of commitment in their future relationships.

Furthermore, educators should encourage open communication and provide opportunities for children to express their emotions and concerns. By facilitating discussions about trust and commitment, educators can help children process their feelings and develop healthy coping mechanisms. It is crucial to emphasize that trust and commitment are skills that can be learned and improved upon with practice.

Lastly, educators should collaborate with parents and guardians to create a holistic support system for children going through a divorce. By working together, educators and parents can provide consistent messages and reinforce healthy relationship behaviors.

By addressing trust and commitment issues in future relationships, educators can help children build resilience and develop the skills necessary for healthy and successful relationships in adulthood. It is through these efforts that we can empower children to overcome the challenges associated with divorce and pave the way for a brighter future.

Encouraging Resilience and Positive Relationship Choices in Adulthood

In this subchapter, we will explore the importance of encouraging resilience and positive relationship choices in adulthood for children who have experienced the effects of divorce. As educators, it is crucial for us to understand the long-term impact of divorce on children's relationships and provide them with the necessary tools to navigate these challenges.

Divorce can have a profound psychological impact on children, affecting their self-esteem, self-confidence, and overall emotional well-being. These effects can extend into adulthood and manifest in various ways, including difficulties in forming healthy relationships. Therefore, it is essential to equip children with the skills and knowledge they need to overcome these obstacles.

One significant area where divorce can impact children is their future romantic relationships. Studies have shown that children of divorced parents may have a higher risk of experiencing relationship difficulties later in life. They may struggle with trust, commitment, and communication, leading to challenges in establishing and maintaining healthy partnerships.

As educators, we can play a crucial role in promoting resilience and positive relationship choices in adulthood. By integrating social-emotional learning and relationship education into our curriculum, we can provide children with the necessary skills to navigate their future relationships successfully.

One way to encourage resilience is by promoting self-awareness and self-reflection. By helping children understand their emotions and develop a strong sense of self, we can empower them to make positive choices in their relationships. Teaching them effective communication skills, conflict resolution strategies, and empathy can also contribute to their ability to build healthy connections with others.

Furthermore, it is important to address any misconceptions or negative beliefs children may have about relationships. By providing accurate information about healthy relationships, consent, and boundaries, we can help them develop realistic expectations and make informed choices.

Additionally, creating a supportive and inclusive classroom environment can foster resilience and positive relationship choices. By promoting empathy, respect, and acceptance, we can teach children the value of healthy relationships and encourage them to build connections based on mutual respect and understanding.

In conclusion, encouraging resilience and positive relationship choices in adulthood is crucial for children who have experienced the effects of divorce. As educators, we have the opportunity to support children in developing the skills, knowledge, and mindset necessary to navigate their future relationships successfully. By promoting self-awareness, effective communication, and empathy, and creating a supportive environment, we can empower children to build healthy and fulfilling relationships in adulthood.

Conclusion: Supporting Children's Resilience and Well-being through Divorce

In conclusion, it is crucial for educators to understand the profound impact that divorce can have on children's lives. Divorce affects children in various ways, from their self-esteem and self-confidence to their emotional well-being and social development. It can also have long-term effects on their relationships, academic performance, mental health, attachment styles, and even their future romantic relationships.

Educators play a vital role in supporting children's resilience and well-being during and after divorce. By being aware of the challenges that children of divorce face, educators can provide the necessary support and create a safe and nurturing learning environment.

One of the key ways educators can support children's resilience is by fostering open and honest communication. By encouraging children to express their feelings and concerns, educators can help them process their emotions and make sense of the changes happening in their lives. This can be achieved through regular check-ins, one-on-one conversations, or even group discussions, where children can share their experiences and learn from one another.

Another essential aspect is providing a sense of stability and routine. Divorce often disrupts the familiar structure of a child's life, and educators can help by establishing consistent routines and expectations. This creates a sense of security and predictability, which can greatly benefit children's emotional well-being and academic performance.

Furthermore, educators can collaborate with other professionals, such as counselors or therapists, to provide additional support for children who may be struggling with the emotional impact of divorce. By working together, educators can ensure that children receive the necessary resources and interventions to address their specific needs.

It is also essential for educators to be mindful of the language they use and the messages they convey. Divorce should never be stigmatized or viewed as a child's fault. Educators should foster a supportive and inclusive classroom environment where children feel accepted and valued, regardless of their family structure.

Lastly, educators can promote resilience through the development of social-emotional skills. By teaching children coping strategies, problem-solving skills, and positive communication techniques, educators can empower them to navigate the challenges that come with divorce and build their resilience for the future.

In conclusion, divorce can have a significant impact on children's lives, but with the right support, children can thrive and develop resilience. Educators have a unique opportunity to make a positive difference in children's lives during this difficult time. By understanding the effects of divorce on children's well-being and implementing strategies to support their resilience, educators can help children overcome challenges and reach their full potential.

www.ingramcontent.com/pod-product-compliance
Lightning Source LLC
Chambersburg PA
CBHW021956170726
47994CB00021B/820